Universities and Globalization: Private Linkages, Public Trust

This book has been prepared by Université Laval, Quebec, Canada
with the participation of UNESCO and
the International Association of Universities.

Published in 2003 by the United Nations Educational,
Scientific and Cultural Organization,
7, place de Fontenoy, 75352 Paris 07 SP,
Université Laval, Quebec, Canada
and Economica, Paris, France
Typeset by Soft Office
Printed by Jouve

ISBN UNESCO 92-3-103890-7
ISBN ECONOMICA 2-7/78-4642-5

Universities and Globalization

Private Linkages, Public Trust

Gilles Breton,
Michel Lambert
Editors

Education on the move

UNESCO PUBLISHING/Université Laval/Economica

Preface

The intricate relationship between globalization and higher education has generated endless discussion and is an issue of debate in a growing number of seminars, conferences and lectures worldwide. Is the growth of borderless education, propelled by distance learning technologies, the rise of for-profit providers and the prospect of the liberalization of trade in higher education through the World Trade Organization a threat or an opportunity for higher education? What is really at stake for universities? Are universities actors or spectators in the new Global Economy? Debates are often heated and consensus difficult to reach.

The present publication, *Universities and Globalization: Private Linkages, Public Trust*, edited by Gilles Breton and Michel Lambert, takes the debate further by drawing on contributions by scholars and policy-makers to a conference on Globalization: What Issues are at Stake for Universities? which took place at Université Laval, Quebec City, Canada, 18-21 September 2002. To formalize the discussion on globalization and higher education issues, UNESCO recently launched the Global Forum on International Quality Assurance, Accreditation and the Recognition of Qualifications in Higher Education. The mission of the Global Forum is to reconcile the interests of national governments, the traditional public higher education sector, for-profit providers, students and the general public, and to provide a platform for dialogue among a wide range of stakeholders. UNESCO's Constitution, often quoted as a charter for globalization, underlines principles of full and equal opportunities for education for all, the unrestricted pursuit of objective truth, and the free exchange of ideas and knowledge. It is hoped that this volume will be of use to academics, policy-makers, professors and learners alike, as it addresses a burning issue that concerns them all.

Contents

Foreword

The idea for this book stems from a response to the prevailing notion in the literature on universities that internationalization is a simple and effective answer to globalization. Indeed, we believe that globalization, which is often reduced by numerous authors to an exclusively economic process – even to the expression of the neo-liberal ideology – is in fact influencing many other fields and, in particular, that of higher education. Our hypothesis is that universities, in striving to 'excel' in their internationalization, do not seem to have taken account of the scope of the new challenges raised by globalization, nor to be aware of the new space in which they will henceforth have to evolve. In other words, the question is whether or not universities have other roles to play and/or places to occupy within this new global social space. Seventeen prominent observers of the world of higher education, sometimes authors, sometimes actors, sometimes both, attempt to answer these questions in this book.* Through a diversity of perspectives and themes, the intention is to provide the reader with as complete as possible a panorama of key questions and challenges at the end of 2002. The debate is structured in five parts.

By way of introduction, Gilles Breton questions whether universities can continue to view the academic world on the basis of their current experience and international practices. He thereby attempts to show that although the internationalization of universities must definitely be pursued and reinforced, globalization raises a series of issues that universities will have to face. This involves taking account of the new sociological, economic, political and ethical issues posed by the relationship between universities in the North and those in emerging countries.

Part One is devoted to the perspective of international institutions, which play a decisive role in the structuring of global issues facing universities. John Daniel, representing UNESCO, explains how education must, in his view, remain a public good (which does not prohibit private sector intervention) while knowledge should be 'made freely available on the Web'. He considers that we are wrong to reduce the contribution of universities to mere economic growth and suggests that their intellectual, cultural and social influence be emphasized. He concludes with a passionate plea for cross-border education, provided that a system of quality assurance and accreditation can be established worldwide.

Chris W. Brooks, representing the Organisation for Economic Cooperation and Development (OECD), sets out a mainly political approach. For him, the issues raised by globalization for the economic world as well as the academic world essentially relate to political choices. To highlight but a few examples, governance, corruption and public goods are key concerns in a world that is seeking new points of reference and in which universities could be mediators between the state and civil society, and the guardians of a new ethics that can respond to the global challenges with the required 'intellectual honesty'.

Lastly, in an analytical summary of the latest World Bank report, Jamil Salmi, representing the World Bank, reveals a major reversal of a trend. Having maintained until very recently that higher education was not a priority for developing countries and its funding should be confined solely to the beneficiaries of such education, the World Bank now calls into question its former analyses and places higher education at the very centre of its priorities. Moreover, it clearly demonstrates the high degree of correlation between higher education – henceforth characterized as vital – and the economic development of emerging countries.

Part Two of the book examines the new global context of which universities are part: the implications of globalization for higher education, the negotiations on the theme of education by the General Agreement on Trade in Services (GATS) and the development of a new mode of knowledge production. Hans van Ginkel points out that the globalization process is not new but is simply much more rapid and evolutionary than it used to be, even in the recent past. In his view, this is a real Copernican revolution since the state is no longer the centre of the higher education system. This entails a complete change of university practices, to such an extent that one can ask: 'But to what end do universities contribute then?'

Jane Knight engages in a very detailed analysis and synthesis of issues raised by negotiations within the WTO on the GATS and explains that no matter what universities think or say, they will have to face these issues or have them decided for them by international organizations. The question is highly complex and cannot be reduced to a Manichean debate. She also addresses the issue of insufficient supply of higher education internationally and, in particular, the difficulty (even impossibility) for some poor countries of coming up with a national solution.

Michael Gibbons then discusses the new conditions under which knowledge is produced. In his view, a globalized world can no longer be satisfied with a mode of knowledge production that is based uniquely on specialized disciplinary approaches. As research problems become more and more complex and context specific, they require multidisciplinary approaches, which he labels Mode Two of knowledge production. He believes that universities have an important, and even leading, role and place in this context, provided that they get more 'institutionally' involved in this new geographically spread and socially distributed process of knowledge production.

Part Three discusses the new role played by knowledge – a subject becoming an object – in societies that are defined on the basis of knowledge. Bernard Pau lifts a corner of the veil on the life sciences. Apart from the explosion of knowledge experienced by biology, considered by some to be the science of the twenty-first century, what is striking, in his view, is its integrative dimension. This means that information is only transformed into knowledge when meaning can be given to it. For him, since global-ization is the imprint of man's hand on earth, it should remind us of our responsibility to the planet. In a society that is increasingly based on knowledge, the onus is on us to show solidarity by making this knowledge freely accessible for everyone.

Riccardo Petrella then raises several questions. Will the appearance of a knowledge-based society give rise to a 'knowledge divide', comparable – through the gap that it generates – to that of the economic society in which we live? Stated otherwise, is globalization not a concept aimed at concealing the failures of development policies implemented by the countries of the North in the emerging countries? In the name of knowledge, will a new 'human divide' be created under the aegis of universities possessing the ultimate knowledge, or will we opt for a solidarity that makes knowledge

Acknowledgements

This publication was made possible by the contribution of the institutions and individuals who became interested in this project more than a year ago. We would therefore like to thank the Comité des Grandes Fêtes of Université Laval, the Canadian Commission for UNESCO, the Government of Quebec, the City of Quebec, the United Nations University in Tokyo and, finally, Université Laval, for their support.

We would also like to thank Michel Audet, Dean of Graduate Studies of Université Laval, for his contribution when the project was first being considered, Eva Egron-Polak, Secretary General of the International Association of Universities (IAU) for her unflagging support from the very beginning and throughout the project, and all the authors who agreed, despite their busy work schedules, to keep to a deliberately tight timetable so that we could all report on a process that is itself marked by rapid change. Finally, we would like to express our gratitude to our translators, Maureen Magee and Chau Nguyen, to Manon Dufour, Anne-Marie Larochelle, Myriam LeBlanc, Nicole Nadeau, Catherine Vallières-Roland, Anne Zylka and all those persons at the Bureau International of Université Laval who assisted us.

Gilles Breton
Michel Lambert
Quebec City, January 23, 2003

About the Contributors

Professor David E. Bloom is the Clarence James Gamble Professor of Economics and Demography and Acting Chair of the Department of Population and International Health at Harvard University's School of Public Health. debloom@hsph.harvard.edu

Professor Gilles Breton is Professor of Political Science and Director of the Bureau international at Université Laval, Quebec, Canada. He was Chair of the Conference: Globalisation: What Issues are at Stake for Universities? gilles.breton@bi.ulaval.ca

Christopher Brooks is Director of Public Affairs and Communications at the OECD. Prior to this he was Advisor to the Secretary General on OECD reform. chris.brooks@oecd.org

Professor Jan Currie is Associate Professor at Murdoch University's School of Education, Australia. currie@murdoch.edu.au

John Daniel is Assistant Director-General for Education, UNESCO. He was formerly Vice-Chancellor of the Open University, UK. j.daniel@unesco.org

Professor Michael G.Gibbons is Professor Emeritus of Warwick University, United Kingdom, and Secretary General to the Association of Commonwealth Universities (ACU). m.gibbons@acu.ac.uk

Professor Hans van Ginkel is Rector of United Nations University (UNU) in Tokyo and President of the International Association of Universities (IAU). rector@hq.unu.edu

Jane Knight is Visiting Professor at the Ontario Institute for Studies in Education, University of Toronto. She was formerly Head of International Affairs in the Office of the President at Ryerson University. janeknight@sympatico.ca

Michel Lambert is advisor to the Bureau international at Université Laval, Quebec, Canada and was the Executive Director of the conference Globalisation: What Issues are at Stake for Universities? michel.lambert@bi.ulaval.ca

Professor Goolam Mohamedbhai is Vice-Chancellor of the University of Mauritius, member of the Board of the IAU and a member of the UNESCO African Regional Committee. mobhai@uom.ac.mu

Professor Teboho Moja is Professor at the Steinhardt School of Education at New York University, a member of the UNESCO IIEP Board and was recently appointed to serve on the Scientific Committee for Africa of UNESCO. teboho.moja@nyu.edu

Professor Bernard Pau is Scientific Director of the Department of Life Sciences at the CNRS, Paris. He is a member of the Comité national consultatif sur l'éthique. bernard.pau@cnrs-dir.fr

Professor Riccardo Petrella is Professor at Université Catholique de Louvain, Belgium, and a Science and Technology Policy Consultant to the European Commission in Brussels. riccardo.petrella@cec.eu.int

Jamil Salmi is Deputy Director for Education at the World Bank, Washington DC. He is also the coordinator of the World Bank's network of higher education professionals. jsalmi@worldbank.org

Professor Peter Scott is Vice-Chancellor of Kingston University, UK and a Member of the Academia Europea and of the Academy of Learned Societies for the Social Sciences. P.Scott@kingston.ac.uk

Craig Swenson is Provost and Senior Vice-President for Academic Affairs at University of Phoenix. Craig.Swenson@phoenix.edu

Professor François Tavenas is Professor of Civil Engineering and Honorary Rector of Université Laval, Quebec, Canada. Francois. Tavenas@rec.ulaval.ca

January 23 2003

Introduction
Higher Education:
From Internationalization to Globalization

Gilles Breton

The primary advantage of the work performed by those in charge of inter-nationalization policies in universities and internationalization promoters is to be found in a field of activity which, while not allergic to criticism, is deemed to be beyond reproach. University internationalization is essen-tially centred on the international mobility of students and thus can hardly be blamed for promoting programmes that allow students to reach out and better understand one another and to acquire international and intercul-tural skills. In the end, these programmes sensitize students to the reality of global interdependence and global issues and, in doing so, groom them to become global actors who will have their say in how tomorrow's world will be configured. Given such a programme, the only criticisms that can be made relate to the choice of the best means to increase the number of students travelling the international circuit, the implementation of safety and risk management measures, and the proposed pre-departure briefings and post-travel debriefings. Thus, one of the essential components of the cultural world of university internationalization practitioners is how to improve student and professor mobility and give this its true meaning in today's world.

The other aspect of international university action obviously involves the internationalization of education itself. This means redefining curricula either through the compulsory insertion of an international component or through the international networking of courses of study. Knowledge today has become so diversified that it is no longer possible for a serious academic unit to claim that it can cover all components of a specific field of study and offer its students all areas of micro-specialization found in a given area of knowledge. Seen from this perspective, the international networking of programmes, whether in the form of mutual agreements, joint programmes, or double diploma arrangements, may consolidate and even enhance student training while facilitating the acquisition of the international and inter-cultural skills needed by today's young women and men.

Such a networking scenario may entail two aspects. On the one hand, we can round it out with sustained efforts to recruit foreign students whose presence in large numbers on campus both ensures a university's interna-tional reputation and internationalizes the campus itself. On the other, we can implement research strategies that extend beyond the mere interna-tional publication of research results, integrating them into networks of international creators of new knowledge. We may then easily claim that the overall results of university internationalization are quite positive and henceforth play an increasingly important role in carrying out the mission of our institutions.

It is therefore understandable that university internationalization is acclaimed by many and, as we stated earlier, is seldom criticized. Indeed, what harm is there in doing good: that is, in graduating students who, in addition to receiving well-rounded academic training, have acquired inter-national skills, opening a window to the outside world, to the campus, its curricula and research projects? These efforts, I believe, are to be lauded; universities should be encouraged to forge ahead in internationalization and even provided with incentives to make this a priority in carrying out their mission.

Yet we must also ask ourselves if these university strategies for inter-nationalization are sufficient and appropriate in the current context of the development of knowledge-based societies, accelerating globalization and greater mobility of human, financial, technological, cultural and social resources. In other words, we hope that this article will provide an answer to the following question: Are we not witnessing a widening gap between the discourse and practices of internationalization, and the reality of the new issues facing the world of higher education?

I would now like to illustrate the significance of this question by making a comparison with international relations. For many years, the field of international relations within political science crystallized the relation-ships existing between societies. However, there are now grounds to believe that one major effect of the globalization phenomenon has been to transform the relations between states into just one system among many other systems of relations created by other globalization actors, be they business concerns, social movements, cultural organizations, institutions or others. To sum up, if the interpretation of interstate relations alone is no longer sufficient for understanding today's world, we must none the less admit that these relations are as important as ever. In fact, globalization simply means a new space in which other social relations are organized and important dimensions of our lives in society are structured; it has not brought about the disappearance of international relations.

I find this short detour into the realm of politics to be useful because it brings my basic concern into sharper focus. Namely, can a parallel be drawn between what university internationalization policies are to higher education and what international relations are to the globalized world in which we live? Do the internationalization policies of universities ignore the new issues raised by the globalization of higher education?

FROM WHAT PERSPECTIVE?

In order to answer this question and all those it underlies, I would now like to describe the perspective on which I have attempted to structure the discussion. The first term that comes to my mind is 'intellectual monitoring'. One of the most valuable contributions by academia to the life of our societies is that it constitutes one of the few social spaces in which a critical understanding of phenomena and the search for the truth can be conducted. In this sense, academia is first and foremost a space for dialogue that is essential to our societies, and its contribution to the public sphere is unique owing to the quality and originality of the projects, analyses and research that are conducted there.

It should be noted, however, that any discussion on globalization today is a delicate undertaking because the word itself has numerous meanings, including many negative connotations that suggest that common sense has been blacklisted, judgement declared out of bounds and reason set aside. In a nutshell, it is an issue that polarizes reductive analyses to extremes and while this is not an original situation, it can, despite everything, prove to be quite useful socially. Indeed, I am among those who believe that the contribution of alternative or marginal trends in the development of our societies is of major importance, because they exist on the margins of institutionalized political society and are therefore at the very heart of the renewal of its agenda. In my view, this is one of the major contributions of the anti-globalization movements since they have revealed the democratic deficit of the process and also allowed the emergence of other forms of globalization such as that of civil society. In the wake of events in Seattle in December 1999, Edgar Morin wrote in the French newspaper *Le Monde* (7 December) that 'a second globalization had been born, rooted in an awareness that control over globalization can only be exercised globally'. He went on to say that this movement associates a deep-rooted, cultural and civilized condition of sovereignty with a true awareness of worldwide problems, plus a renewed determination henceforth to take action for all those threatened by the hegemony of quantification, cost-effectiveness, profit-making and maximization.

I will briefly discuss this much-heralded globalization. I will do this in three stages. I will first present the general framework of my thinking on globalization. I will then go on to describe the reality of globalization in the world of higher education and the new tensions that it generates in this sector. And lastly, I will discuss the status of various projects and proposals aimed at structuring the global space of academia.

A FRAMEWORK FOR THINKING

From the outset, we must not underestimate the extent to which globalization has upset the way we conceptualize reality, casting serious doubt upon a collective concept based on the territorializing notion of our societies. This notion emphasizes the diachronic evolution of societies while relegating to secondary importance the variable spatial dimension, which is viewed as a given. This can be seen in our university curricula in the hegemony of history over geography in analyses of our societies.

To summarize the process, this conceptualization, as it has evolved over more than a century of social sciences and humanities, is based upon well-known reflexes for understanding reality. Our usual way of understanding reality involves cutting it into national portions. In each portion we find a political community – a people, a nation – living on a territory separated from that of its neighbours by clearly defined borders. This community constructs and reproduces itself through its own internal dynamics. At the heart of this self-propelled construction is the state, an omnipresent architect of social order, which alone is empowered to legislate and enforce the law. The state acts as a modernizing force driving society because it is the most powerful organization and the only sovereign power over the territory. In our political science jargon, this is known as granting 'primacy to domestic factors' since it is postulated that whatever occurs outside these national entities cannot be so important as to question the overall equilibrium that the state regulates within its territory.

None the less, social sciences and political science in particular have not neglected the outside world. The division of labour within the discipline has seen the field of international relations take charge of studying the relationships and exchanges that these territorialized communities carry on among each other. Except that here, once again, the state is omnipresent in that the political universe made up of international relations is essentially structured by interstate relations.

All in all, our conceptualization is founded upon two central postulates that I will summarize as follows:

- The territory, as defined by the borders surrounding the state, contains the life of the society.
- The relations that societies engage in are almost exclusively matters of state or, more accurately, interstate relations rather than international relations.

Yet each and every one of us, as ordinary citizens, knows very well that our lives do not cease to exist at the borders of our society. Even citizens who do not frequently travel abroad will quickly recognize that the space in which they are evolving is plural and heterogeneous, and no longer coincides with the borders of the country where they live. The cultural, economic, educational, consumption, intellectual, religious, media, sports and social practices in their everyday lives are a part of social networks that do not share the same socio-spatial demarcation: they may be local, national, continental, occidental or even planetary or global.

You will note that among the practices listed above, those concerning the field of politics have been left out. This was purposely omitted since political practices, being spatially defined, are not of the same nature as the others. We may claim to be citizens of the world but we cannot get around the fact that our citizenship is specifically defined and restrictive. We are Canadian, American, French, Japanese and so on, and as such the territory where we may exercise our political rights and responsibilities is clearly defined. Likewise, the territory over which the rules and regulations issued by the state apply is narrowly defined and generally the state's jurisdiction ceases at the borders that it has itself established.

Basically, this theoretical conceptualization assumes, on the one hand, a spatial correspondence between all the components of life in society, namely the economic, cultural, social and political elements, and on the other, a territorialized concept of the community that inserts individuals, groups and social classes into a clearly delimited societal framework, one which postulates that the territory contains the life of the society.

In the world of higher education, this social conceptualization is traditionally reflected in national university systems that contain university campuses that are territorialized premises. Thus, it is postulated that the campus contains the academic life, since the professor remains the primary agent for teaching and the classroom the main place for dispensing knowledge. One might think that in today's global world, this vision of the university is being put to task because, as Gérard Delanty has written:

Verbal communication is being challenged by new kinds of non-verbal communication and new kinds of agency. The producer and recipient of knowledge are no longer the professor and student engaged in scholarly discourse in the tutorial. Knowledge is being depersonalized, deterritorialized and globalized. It is being taken out of its traditional context and disseminated by new media of communication... In the global age, the scholar's space is opening beyond the traditional spaces of the library, the seminar room and the study into a virtual level. The new technologies of communication have made feasible the virtual university. Whether this is the negation of the idea of the university or a new level of reality with which we have to live will be debated for some time (Delanty, 2001, p. 115).

Why does the advent of globalization upset this way of conceptualizing our societies and, more specifically, the world of higher education? Essentially because globalization is a social process that radically redefines the space for any form of social action and where the compression of time shakes up our notions of the action's place and territory, thereby undermining their reality.

From my standpoint, this illustrious globalization is structured by three factors. First, the loosening of the territorial attachment of the action, whether this be political, economic, educational, social, cultural or whatever; and, second, the creation of a new global space within which new global issues crystallize. The third and last factor is the role of this new space as the new forum for the confrontation and negotiation of collective preferences whose mission is to define this new global space. Expressed differently, globalization is first and foremost an entire redefinition by the actors of their space for taking action.

This quest obviously does not take place in a social vacuum. It is characterized by the emergence of new issues and the implementation of new rules and standards that will provide this global space with an orderly structure. To use the words of the Italian novelist, Alessandro Barricco, globalization:

is not only an extension of the playing field, it also involves changing the rules of the game. Said as simply as possible: The globalized world is one that can only be built by eliminating a non-negligible portion of the rules respected until now (Barricco, 2002, p. 42).

Stated in this manner, globalization is not to be understood as a mere continuation of internationalization. Succinctly defined, internationalization takes into account the state of exchanges and flows that occur between dispersed entities; for instance, the foreign trade between two countries, or the exchanges of students and professors between universities. In Barricco's view, globalization means the construction of a new space that involves the acceptance of the actors who may be on the scene, the issues that will be tackled and the rules that will govern their operations.

I now wish to examine what this concept of globalization means for the world of higher education since I maintain that universities will not be the exception that confirms the rule by being the only actors in our societies not to redefine their space for taking action.

TOWARDS A UNIVERSITY GLOBAL SPACE?

It is obviously no small wonder that globalization has become a critical issue in contemporary university communities. Two major social phenomena, or two major changes, have favoured its emergence. The first originates in the fact that our societies are now organized around knowledge production, having evolved from an industrial development mode into a communications development mode. The immediate consequence of such evolution is that industrial goods no longer constitute the driving force behind economic activity, while the creation of new knowledge products are defining the capacity for innovation in socio-economics. Because of this transition, knowledge has undergone a change in status and has become a commodity that is bought and sold, exported and imported like any other product.

The impact this has on university communities is momentous. The key factor to bear in mind, however, is that in this knowledge-based society, universities have lost their monopoly over the production and distribution of knowledge. Moreover, the presence of other market players enjoying this same production capacity is leading to new university–institution–

business partnerships or strategic alliances. Finally, this has also led to a restructuring of research activities in universities around initiatives that are directly transferable to and profitable in the marketplace, all at the expense of other research whose focus is more long-term and whose economic impact is therefore more remote. In other words, these transformations potentially herald the coming of a new *modus operandi* in university communities, creating new stresses and fragmentation, and these must be assessed and understood.

New information technologies and their accelerated development obviously constitute the second factor that has contributed to the development of globalization in university communities. Universities will be forced into making basic decisions in the near future as a result of the impact of information and communication technologies (ICTs) on research and teaching activities, their de-territorialization as well as their networking, the emerging e-learning global market and the presence of new players on this scene, and the creation of virtual universities, all in the context of a North–South digital fracture (and even within developed societies).

Finally, these transformations, which are clothed in a reductive, trickle-down discourse on globalization that seeks to make the marketplace the organizational focus for all life in society, have contributed to the emergence of practices and a mercantile discourse in universities that proposes the conquest of the education market as the only viable strategy. Furthermore, it is not unthinkable that the current round of World Trade Organization negotiations dealing with the General Agreement on Trade in Services (GATS) and the creation of the Free Trade Area of the Americas (FTAA), including removal of tariff barriers in the world of education, is a major issue that points to the direction of this mercantilization of higher education. We will have more to say about this further on.

These transitions are such that while they make globalization more imposing, they also create new critical issues for universities. I do not doubt our ability to make a rather exhaustive list of these issues. For the moment, however, I just want to dwell on three major critical issues that constitute challenges for the world of higher education.

The first involves the knowledge gap between universities in developed countries and those in emerging ones, which has been widening continuously since the early 1980s. The past twenty years have seen an increase in the number of students attending universities worldwide, but also widening gaps between the percentages of young people studying in emerging countries and those in developed countries. In addition, while there was one doctoral graduate per 5,000 inhabitants in OECD countries in 1997, there was only one per 70,000 in Brazil, one per 140,000 in Chile and one per 770,000 in Colombia (World Bank, 2002, p. 49). In a world dominated by new knowledge production, such statistics understandably become a source of concern regarding the possibility of emerging countries successfully integrating into this new economy.

The second major issue in the world of higher education is the brain drain from emerging countries to developed ones, an issue that university authorities will soon have to confront. The global demographic context, indicating relatively aging developed societies compared with very young emerging societies, cannot by itself explain and justify this situation. Brainpower and expertise are the raw materials that nurture the knowledge-based economy. Stated rather bluntly, we must ask ourselves if, after having guaranteed the growth of developed countries following the Second World War by what some have called the plundering of natural resources in countries of the South, developed countries will now in the early twenty-first century go South once again to loot these countries of their intellectual elite? The relevance of this question can be seen in one example alone: only a third of the 500,000 foreign students who annually attend an American university return to their country of origin.

The brain drain issue raises highly critical questions of ethical and social import. First, it relates directly to the question of the collective needs of societies, whether emerging or developed, versus the development of individuals. This then points to the question of freedom of choice in a labour market of university graduates, which is itself specifically globalized. Second, the brain drain raises the question of the relationship between university systems in emerging countries and those in developed countries. This is especially true since, as we have seen, there is a significant gap between emerging and developed countries in terms of accessibility to university studies and the fragility of graduate studies in certain Southern countries, combined with aggressive recruitment of master's and doctoral students by universities in developed countries. Once again, we must ask ourselves if, in such a context, universities in the South are not just supplying skills to fill our graduate programme quotas without receiving anything in return. In other words, are emerging countries subsidizing graduate study programmes in developed countries by providing them with the pick of their student crop without the universities concerned having to pay the cost of the initial undergraduate training?

REGULATING THE GLOBAL SPACE OF HIGHER EDUCATION?

These first two global issues raise a third concern, relating to the means for regulating the global space of higher education that must be set in place. While knowledge and science are universal, university systems and the organization of university life are regulated by national policies and standards covering – to name just a few – financing, programme accreditation, diploma recognition and student financing. In this respect, the signing of performance contracts between the Quebec Ministry of Education and each Quebec university very clearly indicates that the state – far from neglecting this sector – is redefining its framework for overseeing higher education. The entire problem resides in the relationships between these national systems in regulating higher education while dealing with the global issues discussed earlier. Do these global issues exceed the level of competence of nation-states and do they require the implementation of a worldwide regulation of higher education that would ensure more equitable access to university studies and define models for new relationships in the world of higher education and the interactions between universities?

In other words, we are raising the question of an institutional deficit in the global space of higher education. As in other sectors of activity, such as international law or the environment, must we contemplate the creation of an 'international or global plan' for higher education? Might we not find, in the construction of the European university space, lessons to be learned that could prove useful in the designing of a global institutional architecture?

If globalization in no way lends itself to being reduced to its sole economic dimension, and even less to that of a neo-liberal project, this must not blind us to the hegemony of the so-called neo-liberal project in the organization of new global spaces. Contrary to what a quick analysis of the globalization situation may lead one to believe, when faced with the question 'What to do?' regarding globalization, more than one answer comes to mind. In his book, *Globalization: A Critical Introduction,* the author Jan Aart Scholte (2000) identifies, in addition to the neo-liberal project, at least two other significant political projects: reformism or the implementation of global social democracy, and the various variables of radicalism, whether environmentalist, nationalistic, socialistic or postmodern, that also propose means for regulating the global space.

As regards higher education, it should be noted that there are also highly diversified proposals as to the organization and operating principles underlying the global university space.

To begin with, there is a serious trend towards the commercialization and privatization of higher education via the importing of an entrepreneurial management and culture into the universities themselves, and also through the appearance of new private entrepreneurs who, under the university label, are offering educational products on the world market of higher education. This observation cannot be sidestepped: the spatial restructuring of university actions is accompanied by a market culture that has university institutions exporting knowledge, selling or marketing their expertise, opening campus subsidiaries abroad, developing market opportunity strategies for winning over foreign students and reducing students to the status of client, all within a more general context of reducing tariff barriers and a significant reduction in the state's participation in financing universities. Authors such as Slaughter and Leslie conclude that this commercialization/privatization of universities is part of an even more important structural phenomenon, which is the implementation of academic capitalism.

Others, myself included, are truly convinced of the failings of this project for commercializing higher education and thus are proposing that the global space encompassing university communities be structured around the notion of globally shared property. The negotiation of the very definition of this concept, its financing, choice of priorities, and ways and means for collective actions, coordinating public and private actors, all raise even more critical and highly challenging issues involving the re-legitimization of international public intervention and the need for going beyond the current intergovernmental framework. The enshrinement of higher education in a global project for sustainable human development that would answer the needs of present generations without compromising the capacities of future generations, or even the conception of universities as central vectors for the interconnections between societies also constitute other proposals for organizing this global space.

Obviously, we must draw up the widest range of possibilities for the organizational modelling of the global space occupied by higher education. None the less, the short and non-exhaustive list that has been presented here demonstrates that the debate is now open and that the idea of structuring global space beyond the nation-state – implementing a suitable institutional architecture that will make it possible to define democratically all the processes for decision-making, assessing and legitimizing collective choices within the global space of higher education – quite likely constitutes the most important impact of globalization on academia.

In other words, we organized the conference from which the present volume stems on the hypothesis that the debate on the impact of globalization on higher education needs to be enriched and should not be reduced to a standoff between, on the one hand, partisans of hardline liberalism who preach market hegemony only to come to a dead end when faced with its democratic deficit and, on the other, those with a nostalgic, ahistorical and asociological vision in which the university's mission needs no rethinking or updating and for whom globalization is merely a threat from which higher education must be protected. I am one of those who deeply believe that universities as defined and extolled by von Humboldt and Newman, which were established in the early nineteenth century, are probably no longer a suitable model in the early twenty-first century, but that the loss of the immeasurable humanistic and universalistic values upon which they were founded would constitute an unacceptable setback for higher education and for our societies.

CONCLUSION

I shall close this introduction by simply emphasizing how profoundly I am convinced that globalization has created an unprecedented field of activity for our university communities. It is a wide-open field where everything can and will be done to prompt players to innovate and find original solutions.

The French philosopher Michel Foucault defined intellectual work in this simple and enlightened manner: 'for an intellectual [he said], to work means to think of something other than what he previously thought'. It seems to me that this is the most important impact of globalization on universities: this order that beckons us to rethink the world of higher education and make universities participate in building a democratic and equitable world to live in. In so doing, it is possible that the gulf between the reality of academia and the debates that it seeks to promote on its own role might become that much smaller.

BIBLIOGRAPHY

Barrico, A. 2002. *Next*. Paris, Gallimard. (Folio)
Delanty, G. 2001. *Challenging Knowledge: The University in the Knowledge Society*. London, SRHE and Open University Press.

Scholte, J. A. 2000. *Globalization: A Critical Introduction.* Basingstoke, United Kingdom, Palgrave.

Slaughter, S.; Leslie, L. 1997. *Academic Capitalism: Politics, Policies and the Entrepreneurial University.* Baltimore, Johns Hopkins University Press.

World Bank. 2002. *Constructing Knowledge Societies: New Challenges for Tertiary Education.* Washington D.C., The World Bank

PART ONE

The Point of View
of International Institutions

1. Scientific 'Communism' and the Capitalist Economy: Universities in the Era of Globalization

John Daniel

Scientific communism and the capitalist economy: universities in the era of globalization – what do I mean by my title? It's a phrase that I found in Pekka Himanen's book, *The Hacker Ethic: A Radical Approach to the Philosophy of Business*. He writes that 'present capitalism is based on the exploitation of scientific communism'. That is an elegant way of expressing a tension that has always been part of academic life, but which seems more acute today, namely the tension between knowledge as a common good and knowledge as private property.

That is also the question put to us: 'How do international institutions see higher education issues in a time of accelerating globalization? Are we headed down the road to mercantilism, or are we moving toward human sustainable development, which acknowledges the world of higher education as having the status of a global public good?'

I am not going to answer this question right away. It is a tendentious question anyway, because it expresses a false dichotomy and offers an artificial choice. Let me begin by examining the principles that guide UNESCO in its approach to education in general and to higher education in particular.

PUBLIC GOOD AND COMMON KNOWLEDGE

My first observation is that it would be hypocritical for UNESCO to oppose the globalization of education, because the introduction to the Convention that established UNESCO at the end of the Second World War is a plea for globalization, even though the word did not exist in 1945. We read there:

That the wide diffusion of culture, and the education of humanity for justice and liberty and peace are indispensable to the dignity of man and constitute a sacred duty which all the nations must fulfil in a spirit of mutual assistance and concern.

It continues:

For these reasons, the States Parties to this Constitution, believing in full and equal opportunities for education for all, in the unrestricted pursuit of objective truth, and in the free exchange of ideas and knowledge, are agreed and determined to develop and to increase the means of communication between their peoples and to employ these means for the purposes of mutual understanding and a truer and more perfect knowledge of each other's lives.

I stress three ideas in this extract from the UNESCO constitution: first, 'the unrestricted pursuit of objective truth'; second, 'the free exchange of ideas and knowledge'; and third, 'increase the means of communication between peoples'. These three ideas define a healthy vision of the globalization of intellectual life and echo the evolution over eight centuries of the academic dogma, the academic mode of thinking and the principle of academic freedom.

By *academic dogma* I mean the simple statement that knowledge is important. It is a dogma, because you cannot prove it, but many believe that it is a basic tenet of humankind.

By the *academic mode of thinking* I mean the appeal to reason, the formulation of hypotheses, the search for evidence: in short, the scientific method in the broadest sense.

By *academic freedom,* to quote the conclusions of a conference organized by UNESCO in 1950, I mean the 'right to pursue knowledge for its own sake and to follow whereever the search for truth may lead; the tolerance of divergent opinion and freedom from political interference'.

Are these values under threat today? Should we be erecting barricades to defend the vision of intellectual globalization set out in UNESCO's constitution? In 2001 the *UNESCO Courier* entitled its Focus section *Politics and Profit: Scholars at Risk*. It stressed, of course, the difficulties encountered by academics in countries whose regimes tolerate neither opposition nor freedom of speech.

Most of the articles, however, were about the dangers created by large firms that fund work in universities. This funding often includes tight restrictions, either on the publication of research results or, more generally, on the research activities of the department in receipt of the funds. The authors quote cases where university authorities kowtowed only too readily to commercial pressures. They explained that universities were turning to the private sector for support because of the decline in the public funding of universities in many countries.

I make two comments about this issue. First, preventing the publication of research results is a short-sighted policy, especially for any organization that hopes to take advantage of scientific progress. As Albert Einstein said, 'Restriction on academic freedom acts in such a way as to hamper the dissemination of knowledge among people and thereby impedes national judgement and action' (UNESCO, 2001 p. 20). I also quote Arnold Toynbee who said, in the same vein, 'self criticism and self correction are all too rare in human affairs. They are the sign of a maturity and of a spiritual force which provide hope for the future'. In summary, such restrictions are ineffective in commercial terms and are a drag on human progress.

Some examples of restrictions on the publication of research results on new pharmaceutical products have had wide press coverage. In view of the large settlements made by the courts to people who have suffered harmful side effects from drugs, any pharmaceutical firm has an interest in knowing about all the effects of its products as quickly as possible. Attempting to hide the evidence of side effects would seem likely to increase, rather than reduce, a company's legal problems.

GLOBALIZATION AND FINANCING OF UNIVERSITIES

My second comment is about the decreasing state financing of universities. There is no logical link between the idea of knowledge as a public good and the state financing of universities. Indeed, the notion of knowledge as the common property of humankind was around long before universities received funding from states. There is no problem if states contribute funds to universities, because universities can help nations to achieve certain goals. It is simply a question of proportion.

Research on the benefits of higher education shows that the advantage to the individual graduate is larger than the benefit to society at large. It is reasonable, therefore, for people to pay part of the cost of their higher education. Some object that this will lower the participation rate of people from poorer backgrounds. However, the research, to which Canadian scholars have made an important contribution, shows clear results. In countries with free tuition in higher education the participation rate from people from disadvantaged backgrounds is lower than in countries that combine tuition fees with a programme of grants and bursaries.

I stress that I am talking here about higher education. In basic education – primary and secondary – UNESCO policy, like that of the World Bank, is opposed to direct or indirect tuition fees. This is not a contradiction. The economic, social and cultural benefits that society as a whole derives from basic education are very significant. This is why one of the objectives of the world campaign for education for all, which UNESCO coordinates, is:

ensuring that by 2015 all children, particulary girls, children in difficult circumstances and those belonging to ethnic minorities, have access to and complete, free and compulsory primary education of good quality (UNESCO, 2000, p. 8).

For a concise analysis of the role of the state at different levels of education I recommend Alison Wolf's recent book, *Does Education Matter? Myths about Education and Economic Growth.* One of her conclusions is that we are wrong to promote universities by stressing primarily their contribution to economic growth. She holds that we should rather emphasize their role in the intellectual, cultural and social life of their countries and the world.

I would add that in this era of globalization universities should promote international understanding. Since last year many people have appealed to the 'clash of civilizations' as a way of understanding the current geopolitical tensions. Add to this post-modern attitudes and it is easy to exaggerate cultural differences and downplay the ideas of universal values and human rights.

UNESCO, which like the rest of the United Nations system was founded on the Universal Declaration of Human Rights, viscerally opposes this new cultural relativism. One of our tools is the network of UNESCO chairs and the UNITWIN programme. This consists of 500 professorial chairs in more than 100 countries. They cover the range of UNESCO's interests and topics such as human rights and press freedom.

CROSS-BORDER EDUCATION: QUALITY ISSUES

Another feature of university development in this era of globalization is the phenomenon of cross-border teaching. For students and scholars to be mobile is not, of course, new. Everyone knows about Erasmus, the sixteenth-century Dutch humanist who felt at home in all the universities of Europe. Even before that, English students who were thrown out of the medieval University of Paris for bad behaviour helped to create Oxford University.

Today courses, as well as students, are mobile. For instance, the United Kingdom's Open University has some 30,000 students outside the United Kingdom. Last year I enrolled as a student at that university while being resident in France.

UNESCO is interested in cross-border teaching for three reasons. First, we hope to persuade universities and countries not to make hasty judgements about this development, nor to confuse different phenomena. This form of teaching frequently uses distance education, which still arouses suspicion in some quarters, and often has a commercial flavour even – maybe especially – when the foreign institution is a public one. Furthermore, it falls outside the control of national frameworks of higher education at a time when countries seem to want to control their universities more and more tightly.

For these reasons UNESCO has just set up a Global Forum on International Quality Assurance, Accreditation and the Recognition of Qualifications in Higher Education. Its first meeting took place in Paris in October 2002. The key objective was simply to provide the opportunity for discussion between people bringing diverse perspectives from around the world.

I hope that the forum's discussions will help UNESCO to draw up its action plan in this area. In particular, and this is the second aspect of cross-border teaching that interests us, we want to know whether we should help to develop international instruments to help students and institutions make choices about courses and programmes from foreign sources. Ought we, for instance, to put together a guide to good practice, as was done in the 1970s in response to the controversies about correspondence education? Should we draw up a list of accrediting and quality assurance agencies that meet certain criteria of credibility and rigour?

These are some of the complex questions raised by the globalization of higher education. Until now the accreditation of academic degrees and diplomas has been done almost exclusively at the national level. The most significant exception is the International Baccalaureate. This diploma, covering the last two years of secondary education, today has very high credibility with universities throughout the world. It is governed and managed by an international non-governmental organization. I note in passing that the programmes of the International Baccalaureate Organization are in particularly widespread use in Quebec. UNESCO is proud that it supported the creation of the International Baccalaureate Organization thirty years ago and continues to enjoy close relations with it.

The third aspect of cross-border teaching of particular interest to UNESCO relates to developing countries. These countries react to the phenomenon in different ways. For some it is an attack on national sovereignty. For others, cross-border education is a way of compensating for the lack of higher education capacity in the country caused by insufficient resources.

UNESCO wants to help countries in the second category while ensuring that the mobility of courseware does not create yet another situation where globalization causes money to flow from poor countries to rich ones. In this respect I note a very promising development, namely the notion of open learning material. This is the equivalent, in the domain of teaching and learning of the open-source software movement.

The idea is simple. It is to make an institution's learning materials freely available on the Web. I would have liked to be able to tell you that it was the open universities that proposed this idea. In fact it came from a prestigious traditional university, the Massachusetts Institute of Technology. I see this as the start of a very significant development for three reasons.

First, the learning material that an institution can put on the Web is only part of the process of university teaching and learning. It must be supported by a process of mediation between the student and the material through a tutor or teacher. Furthermore, there is always the need for a teacher to comment on the students' work and to assess their performance through tests and examinations. However, if the world's teachers can access a range of learning materials of quality and adapt them to their needs, they will be able to devote more time to supporting students and less to preparing to communicate basic content.

Second, by exchanging learning materials freely, knowledge can be refined and progressed in an open and collective way, as urged by Einstein and Toynbee whom I quoted earlier.

Finally, open source learning materials are an encouraging example of the basic aim of UNESCO: *full and equal opportunities for education for all, the unrestricted pursuit of objective truth, and the free exchange of ideas and knowledge.*

I am not afraid to call this a form of scientific communism in the best academic tradition that will help the economic, cultural and social development of the whole world.

CONCLUSION

To conclude I come back to the question put forward to us: 'Are we headed down the road to mercantilism, or are we moving toward human sustainable development, which acknowledges the world of higher education as having the status of a global public good?'

I reply by changing a few words. We can contribute to a strategy of sustainable human development if universities commit themselves to the notion of knowledge as a public good and make their learning materials freely available on the Web.

This global public good will help universities around the world, most notably those in developing countries, to improve their teaching while at the same time widening access to it and lowering the cost of higher education. It may seem like a revolutionary formula, but it is consistent with the best academic tradition.

BIBLIOGRAPHY

Himanen, P. 2002. *The Hacker Ethic: A Radical Approach to the Philosophy of Business.* New York, Random House.

UNESCO. 2000. *The Dakar Framework for Action.* Paris, UNESCO. (doc. ED-2000/ws/27.)

UNESCO. 2001. Politics and Profit: Scholars at Risk. *The UNESCO Courier,* November, pp. 6–35.

Wolf, A. 2002. *Does Education Matter? Myths about Education and Economic Growth.* London, Penguin.

2. Globalization: A Political Perspective

Chris W. Brooks

The subject of this paper is globalization, and this of course is a very difficult topic because this word is never defined. To some, globalization is the cause of all evil, including the fact that the kitchen sink no longer works. To others, it is a panacea for a brave new world. Globalization is a process that is essentially about increased interdependence, and a better terminology would be to talk about global interdependence, and perhaps to sometimes talk about global dysfunctioning in terms of dependence and interdependence.

GLOBALIZATION IS ABOUT INCREASED INTERDEPENDENCE

This would provide some focus to and analysis of the problems, which are mainly discussed from an economic perspective. Economic integration has accelerated, particularly in terms of trade and in relation to the traditional industrial economy (the movement of goods and raw materials); it has also dramatically accelerated in financial terms. It is now becoming positive in terms of human mobility and in terms of migration. However, it also brings about a large number of problems in terms of human migration and the willingness and capacity of different parts of the globe to receive or accept people of different religions or nationalities. However, most importantly, interdependence is a question of political independence. We must be careful about the word globalization and particularly about the terminology we use, for we are in a period of mutation, with multiplying uncertainty everywhere. Under these circumstances, one catch-all evil, or one simple ideological quick-fix will not get us very far in making good policy.

It is also important to understand, and particularly to practise and repeat, that this process of interdependence – global interdependence and global disequilibria – is not a choice, but a fact of life. It is something that is here and will not easily go away. It is a dynamic that we cannot simply refuse to recognize.

Likewise, it is important in any discussions regarding what is at stake for universities in relation to globalization to apprehend carefully what is known, at least in the press, as the anti-globalization movement. This is not a movement at all. It is an unsustainable coalition of different interests. Within it, there are two important tendencies, which must be distinguished. The first consists of those who are angry about the distributive outcomes of a global world, and who are concerned about the lack of progress on development in developing countries. They are involved with the equity agenda, and the OECD feels very close to that group of people. We live in a world where results have not matched public rhetoric very closely.

There is a second part of this movement that one could call an anti-modernist movement. We may well be entering the period of the end of enlightenment, and a dark side to progress may lie before us, but to deny modernism would be rather dangerous. In this context, the apparent suggestion by the anti-modernist movement that we have left behind us a golden age, one that global interdependence is somehow closing out, is perilous. Those who share this view should go back and read and reflect somewhat more seriously on our economic history.

Within the group of countries which make up the OECD, it would appear that economic development based on the rules of open markets has actually produced quite satisfying results in the post-war period in a number of important respects, such as life expectancy, education levels, housing standards, working hours, income distribution within OECD countries and income levels. This can be looked at from many perspectives; it would therefore appear that this has been a prosperous and positive period. Clearly however, it is not necessarily one that is going to continue automatically on a linear growth path.

There are two important aspects of the future that must be reflected upon. The first is that it would seem as if developed countries have reached the end of one cycle of development. The twenty-first century will obviously accelerate the new economy and the information technology society, but more than ever it will be the century of biology, and it is here that there will be many mutations, which again bring with them many problems that need to be examined.

In the anti-globalization movement, the reaction towards genetic manipulation, both in pharmaceuticals and in agriculture, is marked largely not by scientific rigour and calmness but by irrationality. In this respect, universities and university academics have an extremely important role to play in attempting to bring about a rational discussion between the affluent world, which may not need innovations in genetics, particularly in agriculture, and a developing world that may be able to profit from them in a fundamentally more positive way. The current climate of suspicion serves as a clear example of the irrationality that reigns in a debate generated in large part by fear, ignorance and uncertainty.

GLOBALIZATION CHALLENGES THE 'RULES OF THE GAME'

From the point of view of the OECD, the critical challenge posed by globalization is to establish some rules, which could be termed the 'new economic and financial rules of the game', primarily in areas such as bribery and corruption, governance, public and private spheres, and trade. The problems of bribery and corruption of public officials in foreign trade must be resolved, and this will not be easy. The OECD's convention dealing with this issue represents a first step in a very long battle to try and introduce some elements of transparency and fairness in the abovementioned areas, which of course becomes very difficult when the discussion turns to issues such as the armaments industry or development finance, as well as other areas of publicly induced trade.

Corporate governance also represents a very significant area, which calls for the setting of new global standards or best practices for corporate governance. This issue has been accelerated by such problems as those that have recently been witnessed both in the United States and Europe. What are, perhaps ephemerally, called harmful tax practices constitute a critical aspect of this work, and essentially involve tax cheating. This is an extremely important area where the rules of the game are absolutely necessary and must be internationally agreed in order to ensure that the rule of law is equally respected by all citizens who have to pay taxes. Unless this work is rigorously pursued, the capacity to sustain government revenues will be seriously eroded.

Obviously one of the current focuses of the OECD is on terrorism, which is natural given the Organisation's membership. However, there are other issues of major importance, such as dealing with organized crime and drugs on a global scale. Therefore, building global rules of the game, or developing what could be termed *soft law*, constitutes the main business of the OECD. This soft law will then of course be ratified, or not, by national parliaments, and it may actually end up constituting the sort of global standards that become ratified around the world in different bodies, and are taken up within different parts of United Nations family.

But a very important issue that the OECD must concentrate on is the organization of a framework through which globalization can be dealt with, within which education will have a major role to play. Kofi Annan helped this process tremendously in Johannesburg at the World Summit on Sustainable Development (26 August-4 September 2002) by providing some structure and focus to the issue of what sustainable development is. His priorities are water, energy, health, agriculture and biodiversity, which are very important issues.

Though there is not sufficient time at this juncture to talk about the adequacy of the structure of international organizations generally, and their capacity to match up to the agenda set by Kofi Annan, the majority would probably agree that the current structure of these institutions is inadequate, and that curiously we live in a world where international organizations are increasingly challenged at a moment when they were never so important. The issues at stake in international negotiations are so important. The OECD will be central in the process of dealing with those five agenda points, and perhaps a sixth (education). This is particularly because the OECD represents 60 per cent of world output and the OECD countries command roughly 80 per cent of the world's economic resources, create roughly 95 per cent of the world's technology and are responsible for 95 per cent of basic scientific research. In these areas, the interaction and importance of higher education institutions in OECD member countries is extremely significant. We must make progress on the agenda set out by Kofi Annan.

GLOBALIZATION IS ABOUT DEVELOPMENT AND SOLIDARITY

The first priority is to put development issues squarely at the centre of the agendas of developed countries. There is too much hype and not enough action, and a lack of the coherence is often found in national policy. There is too much parading along the catwalk and not enough serious attention to the real coordination of overseas development aid and, most importantly, to the conditions necessary for foreign and direct investment flows. But this

– however nearly the target of 0.7 per cent of GDP from developed countries for development aid is met – will not of itself be enough. Foreign direct investment is absolutely crucial if we are to deal with global imbalances because this involves not only the money but also the technology flow, and therefore represents a path on which we must clearly make progress.

In addition to looking at investment capital flows, international trade is an extremely important issue, and developed countries will obviously have to address the question of the opening up of their markets. In this context, agriculture is going to be a critical area that will be a major agenda item, for both the World Trade Organization and the World Bank. If we are serious about global equity, it will be necessary for developed countries to open their markets in order to achieve progress.

Addressing gaps in scientific knowledge is also an extremely important issue, especially in dealing with energy objectives, and there must be no taboos in this regard. What is clear, if we are to deal with carbon dioxide gas emissions and the problem of global warming, is that we have a lot of hard decisions to take. The fact that a serious world discussion of the nuclear option is often pre-empted by remarks proposing hydrogen as a reasonable alternative is an indication of our intellectual slovenliness. Hydrogen is fifty, if not sixty, years away, and there is currently a real energy gap affecting 2 billion people around the planet who have no access to electricity whatsoever. Looking at global energy markets in an open and dispassionate way to see how this could be provided in a manner that minimizes damage to the planet requires a degree of intellectual honesty, and higher education institutions, and particularly academics, must play a key role in this area.

It will also be very important to keep all the players looking in the same direction. We must not let the seriousness of the situation be hijacked. We are in what appears to be a potentially perilous situation because of the multiplication of uncertainty. Keeping actors focused on the same direction is therefore paramount. In this sense, dialogue with civil society is crucial; it is also important that this dialogue be not only a process of listening to public concerns, but also a question of educating public concerns about the real options available, and of trying to keep, as it were, the discussions about globalization in a realistic perspective.

A sixth objective could have been listed by Kofi Annan among his priorities: education. This is certainly the OECD's sixth objective, and the reason why the OECD has upgraded the status of its work in this field. There are practical things that must be kept in mind in an interdependent world. The critical role of lifelong learning is obviously important. The role of universities in *creating* knowledge is well established, and will be even more important in a world of uncertainty. In addition, their role in *transmission* of knowledge is absolutely critical.

UNIVERSITIES AS MEDIATORS

The role of universities in economic development is extremely important as it represents one aspect of helping people to identify with place. Whereas Gilles Breton suggests that we are moving rapidly towards the disappearance of spatial importance – or place – the opinion in the OECD would rather be that place and locality is today more, not less, important. The social inclusion role of universities in an uncertain world is therefore crucial. Universities represent today a mass system: they do not represent the elite system that existed in the past. They play an extremely important civil role: that of mediators between the state and civil society.

Maintaining levels of global excellence is also extremely important. Governments see universities as being one of the motors of globalization. Let us be realistic: they will look for increasing economic returns from education. However, it would be wrong to overstretch the expectations of higher education, in the same way as was done in the late 1950s and early 1960s, when so much damage was done to education in the developed world because it was presented as the way to a new social Utopia. The suggestion at the time was that education really was going to be the vehicle of the new Utopia and a new society, and that all the social inequality problems which confronted our society at the time could be resolved through the expansion of higher education and at the cost of a few additional percentage points of GDP. The deception that followed was very costly.

This question should be approached carefully. It is clear that education is the major residual factor in economic growth. It has a major role to play. It is one of the motors of globalization. But most fundamentally, the role of higher education is to equip society and the individuals within it, at all different levels, with the capacity to navigate through, and make intelligent criticism of, an increasingly uncertain world. This *problematique* will in all probability worsen rather than improve. Complexity will multiply, that much seems clear. New issues will emerge, but our capacity to understand and codify them will become more difficult to master. Therefore, it would appear that this role of transmission, both among university students and society in general, and – in the context of lifelong learning – this helping of people to cope with and navigate through doubt in the global economy, is extremely important.

3. Constructing Knowledge Societies: New Challenges for Tertiary Education

Jamil Salmi

Developing and transition economies face significant new trends in the global environment that affect not only the shape and mode of operation but also the very purpose of tertiary education systems. Among the most critical dimensions of change are the convergent impacts of globalization, the increasing importance of knowledge as a main driver of growth, and the information and communication revolution. Knowledge accumulation and application have become major factors in economic development and are increasingly at the core of a country's competitive advantage in the global economy. The combination of increased computing power, diminishing prices of hardware and software, improvement of wireless and satellite technologies, and reduced telecommunication costs has all but removed the space and time barriers to information access and exchange.

Both opportunities and threats arise from these changes. On the positive side, the role of tertiary education in the construction of knowledge economies and democratic societies is more influential than ever. Indeed, tertiary education is central to the creation of the intellectual capacity on which knowledge production and utilization depend, and to the promotion of the lifelong-learning practices necessary to update individual knowledge and skills. Another favourable development is the emergence of new types of tertiary institutions and new forms of competition, inducing traditional institutions to change their modes of operation and delivery, and to take advantage of the opportunities offered by the new information and communication technologies (ICTs). But on the negative side, this technological transformation carries the real danger of a growing digital divide between and within nations.

Even as these new opportunities and challenges emerge, most developing and transition countries continue to wrestle with difficulties stemming from inadequate responses to long-standing problems facing their tertiary education systems. Among these unresolved challenges are the need to expand tertiary education coverage in a sustainable way, inequalities of access and outcomes, problems of educational quality and relevance, and rigid governance structures and management practices.

PURPOSES AND FINDINGS OF THIS REPORT

The World Bank has actively supported tertiary education reform efforts in a number of countries. Nevertheless, there is a perception that the Bank has not been fully responsive to the growing demand by clients for tertiary education interventions and that, especially in the poorest countries, lending for the subsector has not matched the importance of tertiary education systems for economic and social development. The Bank is commonly perceived as supporting only basic education; systematically advocating the reallocation of public expenditures from tertiary to basic education; promoting cost recovery and private sector expansion; and discouraging low-income countries from considering any investment in advanced human capital. Given these perceptions, the rapid changes taking place in the global environment, and the persistence of the traditional problems of tertiary education in developing and transition countries, re-examining the World Bank's policies and experiences in tertiary education has become a matter of urgency.

This report describes how tertiary education contributes to building up a country's capacity for participation in an increasingly knowledge-based world economy, and investigates policy options for tertiary education that have the potential to enhance economic growth and reduce poverty. It examines the following questions: What is the importance of tertiary education for economic and social development? How should developing and transition countries position themselves to take full advantage of the potential contribution of tertiary education? How can the World Bank and other development agencies assist in this process?

The report draws on ongoing Bank research and analysis on the dynamics of knowledge economies and on science and technology development. Using this background, it explores how countries can adapt and shape their tertiary education systems to confront successfully the combination of new and old challenges in the context of the rising significance for tertiary education of internal and international market forces. It examines the justification for continuing public support of tertiary education and the appropriate role of the state in support of knowledge-driven economic growth. Finally, it reviews the lessons from recent World Bank experience in supporting tertiary education, including ways of minimizing the negative political impact of reforms, and makes recommendations for future Bank involvement.

Although this report expands on many of the themes developed in the first World Bank policy paper on tertiary education, *Higher Education: The Lessons of Experience* (1994), it emphasizes the following new trends:

- The emerging role of knowledge as a major driver of economic development.
- The appearance of new providers of tertiary education in a 'borderless education' environment.
- The transformation of modes of delivery and organizational patterns in tertiary education as a result of the information and communication revolution.
- The rise of market forces in tertiary education and the emergence of a global market for advanced human capital.
- The increase in requests from World Bank client countries for financial support for tertiary education reform and development.
- The recognition of the need for a balanced and comprehensive view of education as a holistic system that includes not only the human capital contribution of tertiary education but also its critical humanistic and social capital building dimensions and its role as an important global public good.

Briefly, the main messages of this document are as follows:

- Social and economic progress is achieved principally through the advancement and application of knowledge.
- Tertiary education is necessary for the effective creation, dissemination, and application of knowledge and for building technical and professional capacity.
- Developing and transition countries are at risk of being further marginalized in a highly competitive world economy because their

tertiary education systems are not adequately prepared to capitalize on the creation and use of knowledge.

- The state has a responsibility to put in place an enabling framework that encourages tertiary education institutions to be more innovative and more responsive to the needs of a globally competitive knowledge economy and to the changing labour market requirements for advanced human capital.
- The World Bank Group can assist its client countries in drawing on international experience and in mobilizing the resources needed to improve the effectiveness and responsiveness of their tertiary education systems.

TERTIARY EDUCATION POLICY IN THE CONTEXT OF THE WORLD BANK'S DEVELOPMENT STRATEGY

As this study shows, support for tertiary education programmes contributes to the Bank's overall strategic framework and goals, as outlined below.

Poverty reduction through economic growth

Tertiary education exercises a direct influence on national productivity, which largely determines living standards and a country's ability to compete in the global economy. Tertiary education institutions support knowledge-driven economic growth strategies and poverty reduction by

- Training a qualified and adaptable labour force, including high-level scientists, professionals, technicians, teachers in basic and secondary education, and future government, civil service and business leaders.
- Generating new knowledge.
- Building the capacity to access existing stores of global knowledge and to adapt that knowledge to local use.

Tertiary education institutions are unique in their ability to integrate and create synergy among these three dimensions. Sustainable transformation and growth throughout the economy are not possible without the capacity-building contribution of an innovative tertiary education system. This is especially true in low-income countries with weak institutional capacity and limited human capital.

Poverty reduction through redistribution and empowerment

Tertiary education supports the opportunity and empowerment dimensions outlined in *World Development Report 2000/2001*. Access to tertiary education can open better employment and income opportunities to underprivileged students, thereby decreasing inequity. The norms, values, attitudes, ethics and knowledge that tertiary institutions can impart to students constitute the social capital necessary to construct healthy civil societies and socially cohesive cultures.

Fulfilment of Millennium Development Goals

It is doubtful that any developing country could make significant progress toward achieving the United Nations Millennium Develelopment Goals (MDGs) for education – universal enrolment in primary education and the elimination of gender disparities in primary and secondary education – without a strong tertiary education system. Tertiary education supports the rest of the education system through the training of teachers and school principals, the involvement of specialists from tertiary education institutions in curriculum design and educational research, and the establishment of admission criteria that influence the content and methods of teaching and learning at the secondary level. A similar argument applies to the contribution of post-secondary medical education, especially the training of medical doctors, epidemiologists, public health specialists and hospital managers, to meeting the basic health MDGs.

THE STATE AND TERTIARY EDUCATION

Research on the dynamics of knowledge-driven development has identified the converging roles of four contributing factors: a country's macroeconomic incentive and institutional regime, its ICT infrastructure, its national innovation system and the quality of its human resources. Of these, the contribution of tertiary education is vital with respect to the national innovation system and the development of human resources.

In this context, continued government support of tertiary education is justified by three important considerations: the existence of externalities from tertiary education, equity issues and the supportive role of tertiary education in the education system as a whole.

Externalities

Investments in tertiary education generate major external benefits that are crucial for knowledge-driven economic and social development. Private investment in tertiary education can be suboptimal because individuals do not capture all the benefits of education. A few examples will illustrate how education yields benefits to society as a whole.

Technological innovations and the diffusion of scientific and technical innovations lead to higher productivity, and most of these innovations are the products of basic and applied research undertaken in universities. Progress in the agriculture, health and environment sectors, in particular, is heavily dependent on the application of such innovations. Higher skill levels in the labour force – an outcome of increased educational levels – and the qualitative improvements that permit workers to use new technology also boost productivity.

Tertiary education facilitates nation-building by promoting greater social cohesion, trust in social institutions, democratic participation and open debate, and appreciation of diversity in gender, ethnicity, religion and social class. Furthermore, pluralistic and democratic societies depend on research and analysis that are fostered through social sciences and humanities programmes. Improved health behaviours and outcomes also yield strong social benefits, and higher education is indispensable for training the necessary health care professionals.

Equity

Imperfections in capital markets limit the ability of individuals to borrow sufficiently for tertiary education, thereby hindering the participation of meritorious but economically disadvantaged groups. Although more than sixty countries have student loan programmes, access to affordable loans frequently remains restricted to a minority of students. Moreover, these loans are not necessarily available to the students with limited resources who most need financial aid. Very few countries have national programmes reaching more than 10 per cent of the student population, and these exceptions are rich countries such as Australia, Canada, Sweden, the United Kingdom and the United States. In addition, where they do exist, student loans are not always available for the whole range of academic programmes and disciplines.

Support for other levels of the education system

Tertiary education plays a key role in supporting basic and secondary education, thereby buttressing the economic externalities produced by these lower levels. Improved tertiary education is necessary for sustainable progress in basic education. The supply of qualified teachers and school leaders, capacity for curriculum design, research on teaching and learning, economic analysis and management – these and many more components of basic education reform are hampered by weak tertiary education systems. A comprehensive approach to the development of the education sector is required, along with a balanced distribution of budgetary resources, to ensure that countries invest appropriately in tertiary education, with attention to their progress toward the Millennium Development Goals.

When looking at the public benefits of tertiary education, it is important to note the existence of joint-product effects linked to the complementarity between tertiary education and the lower levels of education, as described above, and between undergraduate and postgraduate education. While many undergraduate and professional education programmes can be offered in separate institutions (business and law are examples), high-cost activities such as basic research and various types of specialized graduate training are more efficiently organized in combination with undergraduate training. Cross-subsidization across educational disciplines, programmes and levels leads to public-good effects that are valuable but difficult to quantify. In addition, there are economies of scale that justify public support of expensive programmes such as basic sciences, which are almost natural monopolies.

Determining appropriate investment levels

Notwithstanding the methodological difficulties involved in measuring externalities, the existence of these important public benefits indicates that the costs of insufficient investment in tertiary education can be very high. These costs can include the reduced ability of a country to compete effectively in global and regional economies; a widening of economic and social disparities; declines in the quality of life, in health status and in life expectancy; an increase in unavoidable public expenditures on social welfare programmes; and a deterioration of social cohesion. Sustainable transformation and growth throughout the economy cannot be achieved without an innovative tertiary education system to help build the absorptive capacity that is required if private sector investment and donor resources are to have a lasting productive impact.

At the same time, the development of a holistic education system calls for a comprehensive approach to resource allocation. Certain guidelines can be applied to ensure a balanced distribution of budgetary resources and an appropriate sequencing of investment across the three education subsectors in relation to a country's level of education development, pattern of economic growth and fiscal situation. Based on the experience of industrial countries that have emphasized the role of education in supporting economic growth and social cohesion, it would seem that an appropriate range for the overall level of investment in education as a share of gross domestic product (GDP) would be between 4 and 6 per cent. In this context, expenditures on tertiary education would generally represent between 15 and 20 per cent of all expenditures on public education. Developing countries that devote more than 20 per cent of their education budget to tertiary education, especially those that have not attained universal primary education coverage, are likely to have a distorted allocation that favours an elitist university system and does not adequately support basic and secondary education. Similarly, countries that spend more than 20 per cent of their tertiary education budget on non-educational expenditures such as student subsidies are likely to be underinvesting in materials, equipment, library resources, and other inputs that are crucial for quality learning.

The evolving role of the state: guidance through an enabling framework and appropriate incentives

As their direct involvement in the funding and provision of tertiary education diminishes, governments rely less on the traditional state-control model to make reforms happen. Instead they promote change by guiding and encouraging tertiary education institutions through a coherent policy framework, an enabling regulatory environment and appropriate financial incentives.

- Countries and tertiary education institutions willing to take advantage of the new opportunities presented by the knowledge economy and the ICT revolution must be proactive in fostering innovations and launching meaningful reforms in a coherent policy framework. Although there is no blueprint that is valid for all countries, a common prerequisite seems to be a clear vision for the long-term development of a comprehensive, diversified and well-articulated tertiary education system. Student mobility can be encouraged by developing open systems that offer recognition of relevant prior experience, degree equivalencies, credit transfer, tuition exchange schemes, access to national scholarships and student loans, and a comprehensive qualifications and lifelong-learning framework.
- The regulatory environment should be one that encourages rather than stifles innovations in public institutions and initiatives by the private

sector to expand access to good-quality tertiary education. Rules for the establishment of new institutions, including private and virtual ones, should be restricted to outlining minimum quality requirements and should not constitute barriers to entry. Other regulatory considerations should be the development of quality assurance mechanisms (evaluation, accreditation, national examinations, rankings and publication of information), financial controls to which public institutions are required to conform, and intellectual property rights legislation.

- Although public funding remains the main source of support for tertiary education in most countries, it is being channelled in new ways and is being increasingly supplemented by non-public resources. Both of these changes bring market forces to bear in ways heretofore uncommon in the financing of public institutions. New financing strategies have been put in place in the public sector to generate revenue from institutional assets, to mobilize additional resources from students and their families, and to encourage donations from third-party contributors. Many governments have also encouraged the creation of private institutions as an effective approach for easing pressures on the public purse and satisfying pent-up demand.

WORLD BANK SUPPORT FOR TERTIARY EDUCATION

In the 1970s and 1980s much of the support provided by World Bank tertiary education projects was piecemeal, with a narrow focus on the establishment of new programmes or on discrete quality improvement measures for existing teaching and research activities. These projects sometimes created well-equipped academic oases, which tended to become unsustainable over time. The Bank was rarely able to offer the type of long-term comprehensive support for tertiary education that is required for successful reform and effective institution building.

An internal review of implementation experience with tertiary education projects undertaken in 1992 and an assessment of recent and ongoing interventions in this subsector have offered critical insights into more productive ways of supporting tertiary education reforms and innovations. Three vital lessons emerge from past and current tertiary education projects, as outlined below.

- Comprehensive reforms can be more effective than piecemeal ones. Interventions integrated into a broad reform programme based on a global change strategy are more likely to bear fruit than isolated efforts. Financing reforms, especially the introduction of tuition fees and the expansion of private tertiary education, are difficult to implement successfully without equity measures to help disadvantaged students gain access to and afford tertiary education. They also require significant devolution of government control in matters affecting institutional costs, as well as incentives for institutions to engage in cost-saving and income-generating activities.

- The preference for comprehensiveness does not mean that all aspects of a reform should be packed into a single operation. Sequencing provides the tools for responding to and adjusting to evolving challenges. Long-term involvement through a series of complementary operations, as occurred in China, Indonesia, the Republic of Korea and Tunisia, has proved essential for ensuring structural change that is sustainable.

- *Attention to the political-economy aspects of reform is vital.* Until the beginning of the 1990s, little attention was paid to the political economy of tertiary education reforms, on the assumption that a technically sound reform programme and agreement with top government officials were all that was needed for change to succeed. But when it came to actual implementation, political reality often proved stronger than the technocratic vision. In many countries various interest groups have resisted proposed reform programmes. Launching and implementing tertiary education reforms has been more successful when decision makers have managed to build a consensus among the various constituents of the tertiary education community.

- *Reliance on positive incentives to promote change can be pivotal.* The extent to which projects rely on positive incentives rather than mandatory edicts to stimulate change has a great influence on outcomes, as institutions and actors tend to respond more readily to constructive stimuli. The World Bank has had positive experience with such policy instruments as competitive funds, accreditation mechanisms and management information systems. Well-designed competitive funds and incentives encourage better performance by tertiary education institutions and can be powerful vehicles for transformation and innovation, as demonstrated by the positive results of projects in Argentina, Chile, Egypt, Guinea and Indonesia.

DIRECTIONS FOR FUTURE BANK SUPPORT

Investment in tertiary education is an important pillar of development strategies that emphasize the construction of democratic, knowledge-based economies and societies. The World Bank can play a central role by facilitating policy dialogue and knowledge sharing, supporting reforms through programme and project lending, and promoting an enabling framework for the production of the global public goods crucial to the development of tertiary education.

Facilitating policy dialogue and knowledge sharing

Reform proposals that are likely to affect established practices and vested interests are always met with fierce resistance and opposition from those groups most affected by the intended redistribution of power and wealth. Under the right circumstances, the Bank may play a catalytic role by encouraging and facilitating the policy dialogue on tertiary education reforms. This can often be accomplished through pre-emptive information sharing and analytical work in support of national dialogue and goal-setting efforts, as well as through project preparation activities aimed at building stakeholder consensus during the project concept and appraisal phases. The Bank can bring to the same table stakeholders who would not normally converse and work together. It can also share information on a great variety of national and institutional experiences that can nourish the debate in any country and that offer objective reference points for analysis of the local situation and assessment of the range and content of policy options worth considering. This type of dialogue can assist in the formulation of a long-term vision for the country's tertiary education system as a whole and in the preparation of strategic plans at the level of individual institutions.

The World Bank's comparative advantage in relation to other donor agencies in supporting policy dialogue in client countries stems from two related factors. First, the Bank has access to worldwide experiences that can be shared with interested counterparts and stakeholders. Second, it can tie reform of tertiary education to economy-wide reform. The comprehensive nature of the Bank's work allows it to adopt a system-wide approach linking sectoral issues to the overall development framework and public finance context of any country, rather than focus on isolated interventions in support of specific institutions.

Supporting reforms through programme and project lending

In supporting the actual implementation of tertiary education reforms, the World Bank gives priority to programmes and projects that can bring about positive developments and innovations by:

- Increasing institutional diversification (growth of non-university and private institutions) to expand coverage on a financially viable basis and establish a lifelong-learning framework with multiple points of entry and multiple pathways.
- Strengthening science and technology research and development capacity in selected areas linked to a country's priorities for the development of comparative advantages.
- Improving the relevance and quality of tertiary education.
- Promoting greater equity mechanisms (scholarships and student loans) intended to create and expand access and opportunities for disadvantaged students.
- Establishing sustainable financing systems to encourage responsiveness and flexibility.
- Strengthening management capacities, through such measures as introduction of management information systems, to promote improved accountability, administration and governance, and more efficient utilization of existing resources.
- Enhancing and expanding information technology and communications capacity to reduce the digital divide (complementing existing global initiatives by the World Bank such as the Global Development Learning Network, the African Virtual University, the Global Development Network and World Links).

The lessons of recent experience show that Bank support to client countries should be:

- appropriate to a country's specific circumstances
- predicated on strategic planning at national and institutional levels
- focused on promoting autonomy and accountability
- geared toward enhancing institutional capacity and facilitating the cross-fertilization of relevant regional experiences
- sequenced, with a time horizon consistent with the long-term nature of capacity enhancement efforts
- sensitive to local political considerations affecting tertiary education reform.

The relative emphasis and mix of interventions appropriate for any given country are linked to its specific political and economic circumstances both at the macroeconomic level and in tertiary education. Income level, country size and political stability are all important factors. In setting priorities for the appropriate mix of lending and nonlending services in a given country, the Bank will be guided by the following criteria: first, the need to change (the gravity of the issues and the urgency of reform), and second, willingness to reform, as reflected in the government's commitment to implementing meaningful change and its ability to mobilize major stakeholders in support of the reform agenda.

In countries where the need for reform is acute, the choice of lending instrument should be guided by the following considerations:

- Adaptable programme loans (APLs) are preferred in countries with a strategic framework and expectations of political stability, as they facilitate a system-wide, holistic, long-term approach. When necessary, the first phase of the APL could focus on consolidating the strategic framework for reform and on building consensus among all stakeholders.
- Budget support can be extended in the context of programmes for the education sector as a whole in countries where the tertiary education reform agenda is a high priority and where there is a clear commitment from all stakeholders to support the proposed reforms.
- Technical assistance loans (TALs) or learning and innovation loans (LILs) are appropriate where there is government interest in initiating change in the tertiary education sector but the conditions for implementing a reform are not fully met (that is, when there is high need but low political will). Countries should use TALs to help formulate a comprehensive reform strategy and build a national consensus around it. LILs should be used to pilot innovations before they are replicated on a larger scale.
- International Finance Corporation (IFC) loans and guarantees in support of individual private institutions can be extended to complement International Bank for Reconstruction and Development (IBRD) loans in countries that have established a positive regulatory and incentives framework to promote private tertiary education. IBRD lending that involves private tertiary education would focus on system-wide interventions for quality improvement and accreditation (using competitive funding) or for the establishment of student loan schemes for the entire private sector.

Most of the options outlined above are directly relevant to middle-income countries. Important distinctions are warranted, however, for three groups of World Bank clients: transition countries, low-income countries and small states. Such countries operate under special conditions that require a different focus and set of priorities.

- The leading options for improving tertiary education in the transition countries of Eastern Europe and Central Asia include introducing more flexible and less specialized curricula, promoting shorter programmes and courses, creating a more adaptable regulatory framework, and establishing systems of public funding that encourage institutions to respond to market demands for quality and diversity. Other important options include improving access through the provision of financial aid to students, requiring external participation in governance, and professionalizing university administration. Public investments are needed to build capacity for academic and management innovation, to expand the breadth of course offerings at individual institutions, and to create new programmes in response to evolving demand-driven areas of learning.
- Directions for tertiary education development for low-income countries would have three priorities:
    - building capacity for managing and improving the basic and secondary education system, including capacity for training and retraining teachers and principals
    - expanding the production of qualified professionals and technicians through a cost-effective combination of public and private non-university institutions
    - making targeted investments in fields of advanced training and research in chosen areas of comparative advantage.
    In countries that rely on poverty reduction strategy credits, the focus should be on resource rationalization measures to ensure balanced development of the entire education sector; on an effective contribution by tertiary education to the country's Education for All programme, especially through the teacher-training institutions; and on the capacity-building role of tertiary education to promote the achievement of the other MDGs (agriculture, health, environment) and facilitate economic diversification efforts.
- In addressing the tertiary education needs of small states, the top priorities are:

– subregional partnerships with neighboring small states to establish a networked university
– strategically focused tertiary education institutions that address a very limited proportion of the nation's critical human skill requirements
– negotiated franchise partnerships between the national government and external providers of tertiary education
– government-negotiated provision of distance education by a recognized international provider.

PROMOTING AN ENABLING FRAMEWORK FOR GLOBAL PUBLIC GOODS

Globalization and the growth of borderless education raise important issues that affect tertiary education in all countries but are often beyond the control of any one national government. Among these challenges are new forms of human capital flight ('brain drain') that result in a loss of local capacity in fields critical to development; the absence of a proper international accreditation and qualifications framework; the absence of accepted legislation regarding foreign tertiary education providers; the lack of clear intellectual property regulations governing distance education programmes; and barriers to access to information and communication technologies, including the Internet. The World Bank is uniquely positioned to work with its partners in the international community to promote an enabling framework for the global public goods that are crucial for the future of tertiary education.

- *Brain drain issues.* The following measures could be envisaged for dealing with brain drain:
  – increased reliance on joint degrees
  – inclusion in donor-funded scholarships of allocations for purchasing the minimum equipment and materials needed by returning scholars and for travel to update knowledge
  – a preference for sending grantees to top-quality training institutions in other developing countries that possess an oversupply of skilled labour, such as India
  – creation of a favourable local work environment for national researchers and specialists.
- *International quality assurance framework.* In addition to the support provided through accreditation components in specific country projects,

the World Bank will contribute toward the goal of establishing an international qualifications framework through consultations with donors and specialized professional associations, as well as through the Development Grant Facility. Two sets of complementary initiatives will be considered: first, technical and financial assistance to groups of small countries that wish to set up a regional quality assurance system in lieu of separate national ones, and second, support for global quality assurance initiatives on a thematic basis.

- *Trade barriers.* The World Bank will work at both international and national levels to help define rules of conduct and appropriate safeguards designed to protect students from low-quality offerings and fraudulent providers, without allowing these mechanisms to constitute rigid entry barriers. Governments, licensing bodies and tertiary education institutions could apply the following criteria to evaluate foreign providers that are not yet accredited by an internationally recognized agency:
  - minimum infrastructure, facilities, and staffing requirements
  - appropriate, transparent, and accurate information on the policies, mission statements, study programmes, and feedback mechanisms of foreign providers, including the channels for complaints and appeals
  - capacity-building partnerships between foreign providers and local institutions
  - comparable academic quality and standards, including the full recognition in the home country of the degrees and qualifications delivered by foreign providers in a developing country.
- *Intellectual property rights.* The World Bank will play a brokering role to help create and nurture dissemination partnerships among publishing companies, universities in advanced nations, and tertiary education institutions in developing countries. This could be done along the lines of the decision by the Massachusetts Institute of Technology to offer all its courses free of charge on the Web, or the recently announced agreement among six leading publishers of medical journals to give free access to their journals to more than 600 institutions in the sixty poorest countries.
- *Bridging the digital gap.* As part of its strategic commitment to global public goods, the World Bank will contribute to decreasing the digital divide between industrial and developing countries by supporting investments in ICT infrastructure for tertiary education within countries or even in multiple countries, as is happening under the Millennium Science Initiative.

In conclusion, the Bank aspires to apply its extensive knowledge base and financial resources toward increased efforts in the tertiary education sector. Strengthening the capacity of tertiary education institutions to respond flexibly to the new demands of knowledge societies will increase their contribution to poverty reduction through the long-term economic effects and the associated welfare benefits that come from sustained growth.

NOTE

This paper is the Executive Summary of the World Bank report (March 2002) on tertiary education which served as support of Dr Jamil Salmi's presentation at the conference on *Globalization: What Issues are at Stake for Universities?* held at Université Laval, Quebec City, Canada, 18–21 September 2002.

PART TWO

Higher Education and the New Global Trends

4. What does Globalization Mean for Higher Education?

Hans van Ginkel

It is clear that we are entering another period of profound change. In fact, it has already been underway for more than half a century. The idea of this change even manifested itself through art, as can be sensed from Salvador Dali's painting entitled *The Child Watches the Birth of New Man,* dated 1943. In this painting, the 'New Man' is depicted as coming from North America, which should come as no surprise given the period in which it was painted. In it a new society can be seen growing all around the world. The change, however, has since the beginning of the twenty-first century again altered in character. There exists increasing concern about the future of our world.

Widespread, international terrorism, bleak economic perspectives and increasing disappointment with the results of globalization, in particular in the least developed countries, are at the roots of this increasing concern. Despite an upturn in recent years, we know that real per capita incomes in Africa are currently about 10 per cent below 1980 levels. The projected growth performance of the continent is just above 3 per cent a year, barely enough to keep up with population growth. The implication is that widespread poverty will continue to be the bane of the continent in the foreseeable future. This scenario has been exacerbated by the AIDS pandemic, which – without a dramatic increase in efforts to combat it – could take an additional 68 million lives by the year 2020, some 55 million of them in Africa alone. Against this background it seems unlikely that Africa can attain the target of halving poverty by 2015, as called for in the

Millennium Development Goals (MDGs), which were agreed unanimously by all the heads of state in the Millennium Summit of the United Nations. Sustainable development, as was clearly shown during the World Summit on Sustainable Development in Johannesburg (24 August – 4 September, 2002) finds widespread support as the goal to achieve; however, to turn 'words into action' is still difficult and requires a long-term perspective and a great deal of energy and creativity.

United Nations Secretary-General Kofi Annan, therefore, has made strong appeals for a search for ways to make 'globalization benefit all', and UNESCO designated the year 2002 as its year for *Globalization with a Human Face*. It is clear that all education, but in particular higher education, has to play a major role. Higher education in particular, because it plays a major role in training the teachers, and developing and regularly updating school curricula, but also because of its role in training doctors and the organization and provision of health care, and in providing the experts and support for the legal system, the administration, business and industry. Beyond this, higher education has a crucial role to play in sustaining and further developing the intellectual and cultural base of society, helping to preserve cultural identity and give inspiration and justified pride to citizens in the achievements over time of their own society.

We need to ask, however: How is higher education itself impacted by globalization? How can higher education optimize its performance in serving society in our age of globalization? What does globalization really mean for higher education? In my contribution I would like to first analyse major dimensions of globalization, in particular the geographical dimension, before focusing on the opportunities and challenges for higher education it presents and some possible strategies for higher education to achieve its aims better under conditions of globalization.

DIMENSIONS OF GLOBALIZATION

Globalization has increasingly become a complex concept. A framework for thinking therefore must be provided when considering the meaning of globalization. In trying to do so, I prefer to start from three quotations which – when taken together – pretty well describe the situation we are in:

The central challenge we face today is to ensure that globalization becomes a positive force for all the world's people (Kofi Annan).

A runaway world is not a world we give up hope of controlling: it is a world which has introduced new kinds of unpredictability, new kinds of risk, new kinds of uncertainty (Anthony Giddens).

It is hard to predict, especially the future (Niels Bohr).

Kofi Annan is convinced that globalization can and must benefit all people, that it can help ensure a safer world and a better life for all. However, as Anthony Giddens suggests, we are living in a state of continuous, rapid and profound change: a seemingly runaway world. In fact, globalization is a process filled with many uncertainties through which we must find our way. Niels Bohr's comment (taken from his earlier work) seems to suggest that it is none the less worthwhile attempting to predict the future and generate an idea of what is going to happen.

However, when looking at globalization, it is important to remember that it is not a new process. Sometimes it appears as if many are completely surprised and as though globalization has only been around for the last ten years or so, and this of course is not the case. The painting by Vincent van Gogh known in French as *La courtisane* quite clearly represents a geisha. And even though Van Gogh is particularly well known for his painting of sunflowers, he also created a beautiful painting of cherry blossom. *La courtisane* dates from 1887, which indicates that there were already at that time many influences from around the world making themselves felt in Europe. Indeed, it is not difficult to illustrate also – even much earlier – European influences in the rest of the world. Despite these early influences, however, the question is whether or not the globalization we are now experiencing represents something different. It would seem that there is a tremendous increase both in the scale and the pace of the globalization process, the principle difference being that the impacts of globalization are being felt simultaneously at places across the entire globe. It is this simultaneity that differentiates globalization as we know it from the foreign influences of earlier periods. Modern information and communications technology is the key to the present state of rapid and profound change. In the past, the exchange of ideas required our actual physical displacement, and this could only be achieved at a single place and a single time. Now, in contrast, we can interact with many different people in many different places around the world at the same time.

Obviously, one of the major errors made today when discussing globalization is the use of the word itself. Everything that is good and everything that is evil is attached to one concept, which consequently obscures its meaning, and results in it being used in any particular context according to the desires and objectives of the user. In this sense, trying to grapple with the concept of globalization becomes somewhat akin to a skirmish with a shadow. The concept has become completely elusive and very difficult to grasp.

One way to understand the term more coherently is to look at the multi-dimensional character of globalization, or in other words to break it down into its constituent elements. One such dimension is the geographical, which is related to exploration, discovery and colonization: processes we are familiar with from history. Other major dimensions are the economic, the cultural, the social and the political. In discussions of globalization each of these dimensions can be placed centre stage, either individually or in combination with one or more of the other dimensions. More often than not, however, the economic dimension is given the major emphasis. Therefore, it is not necessary to deal again with this dimension extensively here.

The major element in the geographical dimension of globalization is in fact the shrinking of distances. The whole concept of distance has changed in character over time, as has been clearly explained by F. Braudel, a major exponent of the French school of historians and social and economic scientists, the *Annales*. In his magnificent book on the Mediterranean world in the time of Philip II, he focused on the pace and scale of that age. He demonstrated that, over time, the concepts of space have changed in value, using the example of the time needed for a letter mailed in Venice to arrive in London: at least two weeks in those days as opposed to a few hours now with an express service. Using electronic mail we can now send messages simultaneously and instantaneously to many places around the globe. Thanks to modern technology, we may maintain continuous and simultaneous contact with many places and people, and as a result of this shrinking of distances, the frequency and the volume of our contacts have in many respects risen tremendously, as has the frequency and volume of trade.

One of the most important effects of this phenomenon is that we increasingly function at different levels of geographical scale at the same time. One of the earlier scientific leaders of the *Annales* and founder of the French School in human geography P. Vidal de la Blache, introduced as early as the 1870s the dual concepts of the *vie régionale* and the *vie nationale*. Even in those days, life at these two levels at the same time was in fact completely separate. However, in our time, the number of geographical scales has increased dramatically, and many live at different levels concurrently. We can now live and act at a local, provincial, regional, national, international or global level in the same day. What is more, there are networks at each of these levels and, as opposed to other periods in history, people now jump on a daily basis from one scale to the next.

This leads to a third element of the geographical dimension, and that is our manner of perceiving the world. In fact our perception of the world has changed from one involving areas, territories and regions, to another one involving interlinked networks on different levels of geographical scale: of nodes and channels nested in different hierarchies like Russian puppets. A simple comparison of atlases used in a present day school to those used thirty years ago can reveal much about the changing nature of our perception of the world in which we live. We still have maps – nowadays very sophisticated ones – to give an impression of the nature of the surface of the earth, with its mountains, deserts, coastal plains and the like. However, the limited palette of pastel colours that at one time sufficed to denote the political patchwork of the world has been supplemented with maps describing new realities: population densities, channels of communication, sources of energy, distribution of major economic activities and so on.

Most impressive, however, are the pictures from space of the earth by night. The density of artificial light during the night gives a clear indication of the distribution of the world's population in combination with its different levels of living. Of course, there are no borders to be seen; rather, the picture from space is dominated by people and their activities as indicated by the strength of the light generated; nodes and channels of different size and intensity that even seem to ignore political boundaries.

It is for this type of world that we are educating our children and our students. This requires our serious thought, as we have to prepare the next generations for a different world, a largely borderless world, or at least a world in which many borders have lost much of their meaning. A world in which regional integration of countries is on the increase and national governments are ever more decentralizing power and sometimes substantive tasks and responsibilities to the lower administrative levels in their respective countries. The notion of national borders as we have come to understand them is not valid anymore. Even nation states, certainly within the European Union for example, have become to a large extent less relevant in our daily lives, as many decisions tend to be taken at other levels, both higher and lower in an intricate system based on the principle of subsidiarity.

My purpose is not to elaborate to the same extent the economic, cultural, social and political dimensions of globalization, interesting as they are. It may be clear, however, that the geographical and the economic dimensions are strongly related. The shrinking of distances has increased both the frequency and volume of the international exchange of goods, money and information. So has the expansion of free market economies, as well as of trade liberalization and economic integration (on a regional basis or otherwise, such as in the framework of the Commonwealth). Unfortunately, the major problems associated with globalization seem to revolve around trade liberalization and the ways in which trade is conducted, in particular when the relevant institutions are not in place on time, as has been clearly shown by research by the World Institute for Development Economic Research of the United Nations University (UNU-WIDER, Helsinki), among others. It must not be forgotten, however, that trade liberalization has also provided a great many benefits.

It is therefore impossible to single out any one of these elements. It is crucial to analyse in more detail which element of what dimension of globalization has what kind of consequences and how these can be addressed. This is particularly important when discussions turn to the commodification of higher education. In view of the role of higher education in strengthening and developing cultural identities and, for instance, in promoting good governance and democracy, it is equally important to see how through international cooperation universities can support each other.

A COPERNICAN CHANGE

Globalization, most certainly, will present universities with a number of challenges and opportunities. We must try to see what these are and what strategies universities might implement in order to cope with these issues. The logical approach, therefore, is to look at globalization as a complex, multidimensional process in order to understand it better. What can be said immediately is that globalization is occurring concomitantly with the gradual decline in the relevance of borders and with the emergence of the 'network society' as analysed by Manuel Castells in particular. This has led to a Copernican change in the positioning of individual universities. No longer can universities see themselves as only part of a national system, protected by the state which had set rules – often in the framework of their higher education laws – on the programmes of study to be provided and the research to be done. Increasingly, universities must rely on their own performance in order to secure sufficient funding for high quality programmes of teaching and research. Increasingly, they will find themselves unprotected and in a highly competitive world. Even within largely state-run university systems the individual universities must increasingly compete for students, research and adequate funding. They have to strengthen and diversify their external relations with stakeholders, as well as their sources of financing. Consequently, universities must rethink their modes of governance, their financing, their internal structures and external relations, as well as their modes of operation.

Clearly, this statement is especially true for countries possessing predominantly public university systems, where governments set the framework within which universities *must* operate. It also holds true even for private universities, for though they have been left more or less alone to look after their own affairs, they operate within national frameworks and these will not continue to exist in the same way in the future. It is indicative that soon the Japanese state universities, traditionally the more prestigious part of the Japanese higher education system, will be placed at a greater distance from the national government and will become state-sponsored but largely independent institutions.

On the other hand, society cannot afford to lose all control over the activities and development of higher education. The performance of the higher education sector is too important for the future of state and society to let that happen. Society does not only need well-educated specialists in the labour force. It also needs to generate an adequate intellectual elite to reflect on and give guidance to the future of humankind. Society will therefore continue to have a keen interest and direct stake in providing an adequate supply of, and access to, quality teaching and research programmes in universities. Thus, whatever modality is chosen for the organization of higher education, adequate supply, access and quality will always constitute the imperatives for which some kind of solution will have to be found.

With regard to the opportunities and the challenges globalization creates, it is also important to look at how these affect universities in their internal functioning. Internationalization was a key issue for a long time after the Second World War, and many people thought that studying abroad was an important issue. In the meantime, however, it has become clear that studying abroad is in itself far from being enough. This is not to say that it is not important, but it does not in itself constitute internationalization; it is simply part of it. It is, however, at least as important for teachers to travel and work abroad, and it would be well to ask to what point the host institutions, not only the visiting teachers, benefit from this experience. It is rare that this issue is considered from both points of view. Each party must benefit from the experience to ensure its sustainability in the longer term. Furthermore, one might also ask to what extent this experience abroad really impacts on the teaching and research programmes of an institution, or to what extent it truly leads to joint research projects. Any discussion about internationalization must take into consideration these different aspects of the question.

The same is true of access. It is very important that everyone with the talent to study, regardless of his or her socio-economic background, should have the opportunity to enter university. This principle has been adopted, over time, in a number of countries, but is by no means guaranteed everywhere. However, the discussion around access to higher education changes character the moment entrance levels are entered into the equation. Few realize that there is one to two years difference in age – and development – between students at the entrance level in different countries around the world. The boundary between secondary and higher education is not the same everywhere around the world. What happens during these two years? They either form part of secondary education, or part of tertiary education, and this is decisive. Thus, when a country indicates that it wishes 80 per cent of its young people of a particular age cohort to enter 'higher' education, two questions must be asked. The first is whether or not the system will have sufficient capacity. But the most important question is whether or not 80 per cent of the population is indeed academically oriented enough and capable of undertaking *higher* education; and what quality levels should be attained in *higher* education?

A further area of discussion revolves around the relevance of university programmes. UNESCO, in its World Conference on Higher Education (Paris, 1998), focused on four major aspects to prepare universities and higher education in general better for this age of globalization:

- relevance of the programmes (*pertinence*)
- access for all those with the capacities to finish the chosen study programme successfully
- internationalization
- finance.

Other issues discussed included the role of modern information and communications technology, the role of higher education for sustainable human development, preparation for the world of work and relations with other levels and types of education. All of these, however, can easily be subsumed under this heading of *pertinence* (relevance). In a globalized world characterized by ever-greater competition for funding – in particular public, but certainly also private – the question arises as to what universities are really contributing. And as soon as quality is taken into consideration, and accreditation is at stake, there is a whole new series of questions: Accreditation for what? For which qualities? What kind of qualities do we really want? Who will be the gatekeepers of the system? Such questions must be specified and answered before any serious decision can be made. It is in this type of question that international university organizations, such as the Paris-based International Association of Universities (IAU), can play an important and supportive role in the preparation of viable systems of accreditation and the preparation of individual universities for being accredited.

The final issue – directly related to the previous one – is that of *institutional integrity*, which can be discussed from two perspectives. The first is the degree of objectivity and neutrality of the scientific work carried out by an institution that claims autonomy and academic freedom. The second, however, is equally important: given the changes in communication and information technology, there is a great tendency for specialists to create worldwide networks. Does this call into question the integrity of the institution in terms of the kind of integral approaches to major programme areas, which are multidisciplinary in character, that it proposes? In an article on 'Universities: Networks or Barracks?' (1994) I have further elaborated this issue. Will it still be possible, given the state of tension between this type of horizontal and vertical organization, to bring people together in multidisciplinary, issue-oriented university programmes? And this under conditions which make participation in prestigious worldwide – in general disciplinary networks – much more attractive? This is a major question increasingly confronting many universities.

CONCLUSION

When trying to cope with all these challenges and opportunities, it will be highly important to consider which changes in the fields of governance, internal structure and organization, and modes of operation might be possible and adequate. For example, by merely demanding that state-run systems of largely public universities should provide complete staffing tables for the following year during budget preparations or apply for new buildings five years in advance to secure funding, you are not really challenging the leadership of a university to be very entrepreneurial. In other words, each government gets the university leadership it deserves, more traditional and bureaucratic or more innovative and entrepreneurial. The more governments limit university autonomy and take over managerial and administrative tasks, the lesser the entrepreneurial capabilities of the university leadership will be. However, the reality in universities has become far too complex for detailed government involvement in their regular management and administration. Indeed, over the past ten years, even in state universities, the tendency to become both more independent and more entrepreneurial has become more marked. Recent experience in Japan, where public universities have been taken out of the state system and will in the future be financed on something approaching a subsidy basis, illustrates clearly that then the traditional internal structures come under pressure, and an intention to adapt develops. When an individual university must look at the world around it and learn how to survive, a complete change in thinking takes place, which leads to changes in finances, structure and modes of operation.

Under such circumstances, when attempting to address real-world problems, a structure with faculties defined along disciplinary lines does not represent the optimal solution, and simply using a multidisciplinary field as an extra pillar in the edifice is no solution either. The challenge is therefore how to create a matrix organization, which reunites disciplines and problem orientations. In this situation, a time limit must be provided in the internal organization which brings these elements together for limited periods only, in order to prevent the cells of the matrix from developing into new pillars. Such adaptability in organization will help universities to interact more efficiently – in an age of globalization – with other institutions, the world of work and major stakeholders; in fact with the society they aim to serve.

BIBLIOGRAPHY

van Ginkel, H. 1994. Universities: Networks or Barracks? In: *University 2050: The Organization of Creativity and Innovation* (Higher Education Policy, volume 1994).

5. Higher Education and Trade Agreements: What are the Policy Implications?

Jane Knight

The General Agreement on Trade in Services (GATS) and other regional trade agreements are testimony to the increased emphasis on trade and the market economy in this era of globalization. GATS is the first legal trade agreement to focus exclusively on trade of services as opposed to trade of products. It is administered by the World Trade Organization, a powerful body with 144 member countries. Education is one of the 12 service sectors covered by the agreement. The purpose of GATS is to promote freer trade in services progressively and systematically by removing many of the existing barriers. What does this mean for higher education?

The current debate on the impact of GATS on higher education is divided, if not polarized. Critics focus on the threat to the role of government, the 'public good' and the quality of education. Supporters highlight the benefits that more trade can bring in terms of innovations through new providers and delivery modes, greater student access and increased economic gain. Trade liberalization has the potential to change profoundly the nature and provision of higher education and the role that government plays in that provision. The purpose of this paper is to discuss both the risks and opportunities that GATS brings to higher education and to identify some of the policy implications and issues that need further analysis.

CHANGES AND CHALLENGES IN THE PROVISION OF HIGHER EDUCATION

The promotion of trade in education services is directly linked to a number of significant trends in higher education. These include:

- the emergence of new for-profit education providers
- the growth of alternate electronic delivery modes both domestically and internationally
- the response to the labour market
- the increase in international academic mobility of students, professors and programmes
- the limited budget capacity (or political will) of government to meet the increasing domestic demand for higher education.

In short, these trends are contributing to, as well as responding to, the expanding business of cross-border delivery of higher education services. GATS aims to capitalize on this market potential and promote further international trade in education services by establishing rules and procedures to eliminate barriers to trade.

The demand for higher and adult education, especially for professionally related courses, is increasing in most countries for a number of reasons: the growth of the knowledge economy, a movement to lifelong learning and changing demographics. While demand is growing, the capacity of the public sector to satisfy the demand is being challenged. This is due to budget limitations, the changing role of government and increased emphasis on market economy and privatization.

The unmet demand for higher education has paved the way for new types of providers such as corporate universities, for-profit institutions, media companies, education brokers and private universities (CVCP, 2000, p. 30). It should be noted that private universities have a long history in countries such as Japan, Chile and the United States, but for the majority of countries private providers are a relatively new phenomenon. There are mixed reactions to these new private providers, especially those that are profit driven. While it is dangerous to overgeneralize, it is fair to say that the traditional public institutions have expressed concern about the quality of education, consumer protection and fee structures of some of these for-profit providers.

Corporate universities are also a relatively new phenomenon. They are popular in the United States, where the numbers have grown from 400 in 1988 to 1,600 in 1998 (Corporate University Xchange, 1999). These entities specialize in technical training and professional development courses and are competing with the continuing and professional education units of public institutions. They recognize the value of investing in new learning and teaching strategies and give priority to consumer service. These providers are voluntarily entering the education and training market, and in some cases are being supported by the government with the expectation that they will bring innovation through competition to the education sector/industry.

At the same time, innovations in information and communication technologies (ICTs) are providing alternate and virtual ways to deliver higher education. Alternative types of cross-border programme delivery such as branch campuses, e-learning, virtual universities, franchise and twinning arrangements are being developed (Cunningham et al., 2000). Many new private providers are adopting non-traditional forms of delivery especially across national borders. New technologies have made Internet-based learning possible and popular. As a result virtual universities are being developed, with Phoenix University, owned and operated by Apollo Corporation, the best known and most successful in competing for market share.

Public institutions are also becoming more involved in transnational education and are setting up satellite campuses and learning centres in foreign countries. This is an interesting phenomenon because as soon as public institutions cross a national border they are usually defined as private providers in that host country (Davis et al., 2000). In most cases, the establishment of offshore locations and franchise arrangements are driven by income-generating rationales and thus entail a new kind of hybrid institution, which is a public provider at home and a private provider in a foreign country. Monash University in Australia has recently established branch campuses in Malaysia and South Africa and is intending to create a global network of public/private institutions. This is an especially interesting situation, and it is a signal of future development in terms of the privatization and marketization of higher education at home and across borders.

The scenario of higher education provision is changing as providers – public and private, new and traditional – are delivering education services across national borders to meet needs in other countries. As a result, an exciting but rather complex, picture of higher education provision is emerging.

It is important to ask 'so what?'. Many educators would point out that demand for higher education has been steadily increasing for years and that the academic mobility of students, scholars, teachers and knowledge has been an integral aspect of higher education for centuries. This is true. But the picture is changing. Now, not only are more people moving, but academic programmes and providers are also moving across borders. More and more, economic rationales and benefits are driving a large part of the international or cross-border supply of education. This profit motive is a reality today, and applies to both private providers and in some cases public institutions. In short, the business or commercial side of education is growing.

A recent OECD study (Larsen et al., 2001, p.3) estimated that the value of trade in education services was about US$30 billion in 1999. In fact, because this figure only includes students studying abroad and does not include other types of cross-border education, it represents only a portion of the current level of trade. The future market is growing and this is one reason why education is one of the major sectors targeted by GATS. It is therefore important that educators are cognizant of the impact of trade liberalization on higher education and are taking steps to maximize the benefits and opportunities, and at the same time, minimize the threats to a robust and quality higher education system.

Figure 5.1 presents some of the key terms that are used in this paper. Given the changes in higher education, there is a plethora of new terms coming on the scene. This illustrates the complexity of higher education provision, but also leads to confusion, misunderstanding and perhaps some hot debate around trade liberalization and education.

The next section of the paper focuses on GATS and in particular on how the education service sector is defined and regulated by the rules and obligations inherent in the agreement.

STRUCTURE AND PURPOSE OF GATS

GATS is the first ever set of multilateral rules covering international trade in services. The agreement has three parts. The first part is the framework containing the general principles and rules. The second part consists of the national schedules, which list the countries' specific commitments on access to their domestic market by foreign providers. The third part consists of annexes that detail specific limitations for each sector and are attached to the schedule of commitments. To understand GATS, it is essential to understand what kind of education services will be covered by it and what is meant by higher education services.

The agreement defines four ways in which a service can be traded, known as 'modes of supply' (WTO, 1998, p.6). These four modes of trade apply to all service sectors in GATS. Figure 5.2 provides a generic definition for each mode, applies them to the education sector and comments on the relative size of the market supply and demand.

Trade in education is organized into five categories of service according to the UN Provisional Central Classification. They are Primary, Secondary, Higher, Adult and Other. The last three are of particular interest to this paper. Clarification is needed to determine what is included in each group, especially the 'Other' services group. At this time it is wide open and includes services as diverse as language testing, student recruitment and quality assessment of programmes.

Three major principles

The overall framework contains a number of general obligations applicable to all trade in services regardless of whether a country has made a specific commitment to sectors or not. These are called unconditional obligations. There are three that are fundamental to this discussion. The Most Favoured Nation (MFN) rule requires equal and consistent treatment of all foreign trading partners. It means treating one's trading partners equally. Under GATS, if a country allows foreign competition in a sector, equal opportunities in that sector should be given to service providers from all WTO members. This also applies to mutual exclusion treatment. For

Figure 5.1. Definition of Terms

Cross-border delivery of higher education services

Transnational education: All types of higher education study where the learners are located in a country different from the one where the awarding institution is based (Expert Meeting…, 2001, p. 8).

Borderless education: Education initiatives which cross the traditional borders of higher education, whether geographical or conceptual (CVCP, 2000, p. 7).

Cross-border education: A generic term to describe the delivery of education where the teacher, learner, programme, institution or course materials cross a national jurisdictional border.

Trade in education services

Trade in education services: The delivery of education services across jurisdictional borders for commercial purposes or economic gain.

Trade liberalization: The promotion of increased trade through the removal of barriers that impede freer trade. Trade agreements such as GATS, NAFTA, EU and APEC are legal entities with formal rules and obligations designed to liberate trade systematically from current barriers or impediments.

Cross-border providers and methods of delivery of higher education services

Concept/term	Type	Example
New private for-profit providers	Corporate universities	Cisco, IBM
	For-profit private institutions	Devry Institute
Includes a diverse range of non-governmental bodies, institutions, companies	Media companies	Thompson Learning
	Educational brokers	UK Open Learning Foundation
	University consortia*	Universitas
	Professional bodies*	Australia's Association of Professional Engineers

*May also engage in non-profit education services.

New and non-traditional delivery methods	Open/distance and E-learning	Athabasca University
	Virtual universities	Phoenix University*
Delivered by private and public institutions within a country and across borders	Franchises	Informatics Ltd*
	Satellite campuses	RMIT University in Viet Nam*
	Twinning arrangements	Sunway College Malaysia*

*Private for-profit providers.

Policy implications of trade or cross-border education with new for-profit providers and non-traditional delivery methods

Funding (public): Financial support from public governmental sources for providers of higher education (i.e. operating grants) or for students (i.e. loans, bursaries)

Access: Ability of learners to have fair and equitable opportunities to access higher education services.

Regulation: Licensing agreements for new private providers and transnational/ foreign providers to operate

Accreditation: Recognition whether an institution/provider qualifies for a certain status by meeting agreed standards of quality.

Quality assurance: A process to assess and assure that an institution, provider or programme continues to meet specific standards. Used for improvement and accountability purposes.

Figure 5.2. Mode of Supply

	Explanation	Examples in higher education	Size/potential of market
1. Cross-border Supply	The provision of a service where the service crosses a border (does not require the physical movement of the consumer)	Distance education e-learning Virtual universities	Currently a relatively small market Seen to have great potential through the use of new ICTs and especially the Internet
2. Consumption abroad	Provision of the service involving the movement of the consumer to the country of the supplier	Students who go to another country to study	Currently represents the largest share of the global market for education services
3. Commercial presence	The service provider establishes or has presence of commercial facilities in another country in order to render service	Local branch or satellite campuses Twinning partnerships Franchising arrangements with local institutions	Growing interest and strong potential for future growth Most controversial as it appears to set international rules on foreign investment
4. Presence of natural persons	Persons travelling to another country on a temporary basis to provide service	Professors, teachers, researchers working abroad	Potentially a strong market given the emphasis on mobility of professionals

instance, if a foreign provider establishes a branch campus in Country A, then Country A must permit all WTO members the same opportunity/treatment. Or if Country A chooses to exclude Country B from providing a specific service, then all WTO members are excluded. This may apply even if the country has made no specific commitment to provide foreign access to its markets. Therefore, MFN has implications for those countries that are already engaged in trade in educational services and/or provide access to foreign education providers.

MFN is not the same as National Treatment, which requires equal treatment for foreign providers and domestic providers. Once a foreign supplier has been allowed to supply a service in a country there should be no discrimination in treatment between the foreign and domestic providers. It is important to note that this only applies where a country has made a specific commitment and exemptions are allowed. It is the national treatment principle that GATS' critics believe can put education as a 'public good' at risk.

The third important element is Market Access. This relates to the degree to which market access is granted to foreign providers in specified sectors. Each country determines limitations on market access for each committed sector and lists in its national schedules those services for which it wishes to provide access to foreign providers. In addition to choosing which service sector/s will be committed, each country determines the extent of commitment by specifying the level of market access and the degree of national treatment they are prepared to guarantee.

GATS is described as a voluntary agreement because countries can decide which sectors they will agree to come under its rules. This is done through the preparation of their national schedules of commitments and through the 'request–offer' negotiation rounds. However, there are aspects of the agreement that call its voluntary nature into question, notably the built-in progressive liberalization agenda. There are several aspects of GATS that are highly controversial and require the serious attention of the higher education sector. These worrisome issues are briefly introduced in the following section.

Which education services are covered or exempted?

Probably the most controversial and critical issue related to the agreement is the meaning of Article 1.3 (AUCC, 2001), which defines the services that are covered or exempted. According to the WTO, the agreement is deemed to apply to all measures affecting services *except* 'those services supplied in the exercise of governmental authority'. GATS supporters (Ascher, 2001) maintain that education provided and funded by the government is therefore exempt. Sceptics question the broad interpretation of the clause and ask for a more detailed analysis. The agreement states that 'in the exercise of governmental authority' means the service is provided on a 'non-commercial basis' and 'not in competition' with other service suppliers. These are the core issues at the heart of much of the debate about which services are covered.

Education critics of the GATS maintain that, due to the wide-open interpretation of 'non-commercial' and 'not in competition' terms, the public sector/government service providers may not in fact be exempt (Cohen, 2000). The situation is especially complicated in those countries where there is a mixed public–private higher education system, or where a significant amount of funding for public institutions is in fact coming from the private sector, or where so called public institutions are providing privatized programmes. Another complication is that a public education institution in an exporting country is often defined as private/commercial when it crosses the border and delivers in the importing country. Therefore, one needs to question what 'non-commercial' really means in terms of higher education trade.

The debate about what 'not in competition' means is fuelled by the fact that there does not appear to be any qualification or limit on the term (Gottlieb and Pearson, 2001). For instance, if non-government providers (private non-profit or commercial) are delivering services, are they deemed to be in competition with government provision? In this scenario, public providers may be defined as being 'in competition' by the mere existence of non-governmental operators. Does the method of delivery influence or limit the concept of 'in competition'? Does the term cover only situations where there is a similar mode of delivery or, for instance, does this term mean that public providers using traditional face-to-face classroom methods could be seen to be competing with foreign for-profit e-learning providers? These are unanswered questions that need clarification.

Supporters of GATS emphasize that education is to a large extent a government function and that the agreement does not seek to displace the public education systems and the right of government to regulate and meet domestic policy objectives. Critics express concern that the whole question of the protection of public services is very uncertain and potentially at risk by the narrow interpretation of what governmental authority means and a wide-open interpretation of what 'not in competition' and 'non-commercial basis' mean. Clearly, the question – which higher and adult education 'services exercised in governmental authority' are exempt from GATS – needs to be at the centre of the debate on the risks and opportunities associated with the agreement. Further and immediate action is required to gain clarification of which higher education providers or services are exempt. The higher education sector is not the only sector that has been troubled by the ambiguity of Clause 1.3. For instance, the financial services sector took an important step and prepared two annexes to the agreement that spelled out what was meant by financial services and, second, delineated which were considered to be 'those services supplied in the exercise of governmental authority'. This is a constructive and concrete step that the higher education sector, or perhaps the entire education sector, needs to consider.

What does the principle of progressive liberalization mean?

GATS is not a neutral agreement as it aims to promote and enforce the liberalization of trade in services. The process of progressive liberalization involves two aspects: extending GATS coverage to more service sectors, and decreasing the number and extent of measures that serve as impediments to increased trade. Therefore, in spite of the right of each country to determine the extent of its commitments, with each new round of negotiations countries are expected to add sectors or subsectors to their national schedules of commitments and to negotiate the further removal of limitations on market access and national treatment (AUCC, 2001).

The intention of GATS is to facilitate and promote more opportunities for trade. Therefore, countries that are not interested in either the import or export of education services will most likely experience greater pressures to allow market access to foreign providers. GATS is a very new instrument and it is too soon to predict the reality or extent of these potential opportunities or risks.

How are subsidies treated under GATS?

Subsidies are considered to be 'measures' under the GATS. As a result, under MFN treatment, when a specific commitment is made, it implies that if a subsidy is granted to one foreign service provider, then it must be granted to all foreign providers. Similarly, under national treatment, if a country decides to make a commitment, then any subsidies given to domestic providers must also be given to foreign providers (except where a country imposes special limitations on national treatment) (Sinclair, 2000). This can have significant implications for public-funded provision as it would remove the ability of government to give preferential treatment to domestic providers. One can ask whether, if this scenario were taken to its extreme, public funding for higher education would be subject to action under GATS as an unfair subsidy (AUCC, 2001). The ruling on subsidies is the subject of much debate and continuing work at the WTO. Educators also need to focus attention on how the issue of subsidies applies to and impacts upon education services, including the important area of research and development services.

These issues relate to the mechanics and legalities of the agreement itself. In addition, there are other aspects of the GATS that are controversial and need further analysis. These include the dispute mechanism and treatment of monopolies, for example. It must be remembered that GATS is still an untested agreement and a certain amount of confusion exists on how to interpret the major rules and obligations. It took many years to iron out the inconsistencies in the General Agreement on Tariffs and Trade and the same will likely be true for GATS. While trade specialists and lawyers need to review the technical and legal aspects of the agreement, it is educators who need to study how the agreement applies to and affects education services.

EXTENT OF COUNTRY COMMITMENTS

The education sector is one of the least committed sectors. The reason is not clear, but perhaps it can be attributed to the need for countries to strike a balance between pursuing domestic education priorities and exploring ways in which trade in education services can be further liberalized. Or it could be linked to the fact that to date education has had a very low priority in the major bilateral/regional trade agreements and, rightly or wrongly, the same may be true for GATS.

Only 44 of the 144 WTO Members have made commitments to education, and only 21 of these have included commitments to higher education (WTO, 2000). It is interesting to note that Congo, Lesotho, Jamaica and Sierra Leone have made full unconditional commitments to higher education, perhaps with the interest and intent of encouraging foreign providers to help develop their education systems. Australia's commitment for higher education covers provision of private tertiary education services including those at the university level. The European Union has included higher education in their schedule, with some limitations on all modes of trade except 'consumption abroad', which generally means foreign tuition-paying students. To date, only four (the United States, New Zealand, Australia and Japan) of the twenty-one countries with higher education commitments have submitted a negotiating proposal outlining their interests and issues. All requests for liberalization of trade were due in June 2002. It should be noted that these were bilateral requests and are not required to be made public. The response to these requests, known as offers, were due in January 2003. This is a critical time for educators to be in close contact with the government and for trade officials to ensure that their opinions and expertise are heard.

Further analysis of the factors driving commitments or the lack of commitments in higher education is needed. There are diverse perspectives on the number and substance of commitments because countries have different national policy objectives and therefore different goals and expectations from trade in education services.

Different rationales and approaches exist. For example, a consumer-oriented rationale can be interpreted as the need to provide a wider range of opportunities to consumers or the need to protect consumers by assuring appropriate levels of access to and quality of education services. The economic rationale can be understood as a way to increase trade revenues for exporting countries, or as a means to attract additional investment for education for importing countries. Other see the economic rationale as sabotaging the social development goals of education or even the scientific and knowledge purposes. Any number of issues can be used to illustrate the dichotomy of opinions on the rationales and benefits of increased trade in education. Different opinions exist between and within countries, and certainly among education groups as well. Further debate and analysis is necessary so that an informed position is taken on why trade liberalization is or is not attractive to an individual country, and how trade agreements help or hinder the achievement of national goals and global interests.

DEVELOPING COUNTRY INTERESTS

The voices of developing countries need to be heard so that the benefits and risks associated with increased trade are clear and do not undermine their own efforts to develop and enhance their domestic higher education systems. However, the voices and interests of the developing countries differ. The opportunity to have foreign suppliers provide increased access to higher and adult education programmes, or to invest in the infrastructure for education provision, is attractive to some. The fear of foreign dominance or exploitation of a national system and culture is expressed by others. Trade liberalization 'for whose benefit' or 'at what cost' are key questions.

Quality and accreditation are at the heart of this debate. The importance of frameworks for licensing, accreditation, qualification recognition and quality assurance are important for all countries, whether they are importing or exporting education services. Developing countries have expressed concern about their capacity to have such frameworks in place in light of the push toward trade liberalization and increased cross-border delivery of education (Singh, 2001).

GATS is one of many factors or instruments that are encouraging greater mobility of professions. Although the agreement focuses on temporary movements of the labour force, it may lead to and facilitate permanent migration as well. The implications from increased mobility of teachers and researchers are particularly relevant to developing countries. It will be a major challenge to improve education systems if well-qualified professionals and graduates are being attracted to positions in other countries.

At the root of the question about the impact of GATS on developing countries is the fundamental issue of their capacity to participate effectively in the global trading system and to be equal members in the WTO. Strong sentiments exist about the potential for trade rules to make poor countries poorer instead of narrowing the gap between developed and developing countries. The perceived injustice regarding the expectation that poor nations should remove trade barriers while rich nations retain barriers on certain goods contributes to the strong reactions of some developing countries about GATS in general.

The issue of barriers is fundamental because it is the elimination of these impediments that is the *raison d'être* of GATS. There are some barriers that are applicable to all sectors, and others that are specific to the education services sector. There is no agreement or consensus on which are the most critical as they are usually seen from a self-interest perspective. Attention needs to be given to whether the barriers are seen from the perspective of an exporting or importing country. Finally, it is important to remember that what is perceived as a barrier by some countries is in fact a fundamental regulation or aspect of the education system in another country (Cohen, 2000).

TRADE LIBERALIZATION AND TRENDS IN HIGHER EDUCATION

Trade liberalization is firmly enmeshed with other issues and trends in higher education and it is therefore challenging to isolate implications emanating from trade alone. These trends include:

- the use of information and communication technologies (ICTs) for domestic and cross-border delivery of programmes
- the growing number of private for-profit entities providing higher education opportunities domestically and internationally
- the increasing costs and tuition fees faced by students of public (and private) institutions
- the need for public institutions to seek alternate sources of funding, which sometimes means engaging in for-profit activities or seeking private sector sources of financial support

- the ability (or inability) of government to fund the increasing demand for higher and adult education.

These trends are evident in both developed and, to some extent, developing countries. How does the existence of GATS relate to these trends? While it may contribute to more commercial or market-oriented approaches to education and lead to expanded use of electronic education, it cannot be held responsible for the emergence of these trends. In fact, it is important to acknowledge that the business side of transnational or cross-border education was alive and well before the advent of GATS. Supporters of more trade in education services celebrate the existence of the agreement as a means to maximize the benefits of these trends and new opportunities. Critics, on the other hand, emphasize the risks associated with increased trade, believing that it leads to more for-profit providers, to programmes of questionable quality and to a market oriented approach – all of which are seen to challenge the traditional notion of education as a 'public good' (Nunn, 2001*b*).

POLICY ISSUES AND QUESTIONS

This section identifies questions and issues that need to be explored in terms of the impact of trade liberalization and GATS on policy directions for higher education.

Role of government

The changing role of government is one of the most contentious issues. First, let it be said that in general globalization and the new public management approach are challenging and changing roles of government and of the nation state (Held et al., 1999). The movement toward more trade liberalization is yet another factor. With respect to education, the government usually plays a role in the funding, regulating, monitoring and delivery of higher education, or at least designates bodies to do so. This is true in countries where a public system dominates or where a mixed public/private system exists (AUCC et al., 2001).

A combination of increased demand for public services and limited financial capacity is forcing governments to examine their priorities and options for service delivery. In higher education, it is resulting in a number of new developments. These include:

- developing funding formulas that are placing more of the financial burden on students
- forcing publicly funded institutions to seek alternate and additional sources of funds through entrepreneurial or commercial activities at home and abroad
- individual institutions wanting increased autonomy from government regulations
- permitting new private providers (non-profit and for-profit) to deliver specific education and training programmes.

These developments are further complicated if and when a foreign public or private education provider is interested in access to the domestic market and/or if a domestic public provider is interested in seeking markets in other countries. Together these scenarios require the government to take a long-term and macro perspective on the advantages and disadvantages of increased foreign trade on their role in the provision and regulation of higher education.

Student access

Government and public education institutions have long felt a responsibility for ensuring access to education opportunities for the student population. In many if not most countries, this is a challenging issue as the demand for higher and adult education is steadily growing, often beyond the capacity of the country to provide it. This is one more reason why some students are interested in out-of-country education opportunities and more providers are prepared to offer higher education services across borders.

When increased trade liberalization is factored into this scenario the question of access becomes complicated. Advocates of liberalized trade maintain that consumers/students can have greater access to a wider range of education opportunities at home and abroad (APEC, 2001). Non-supporters of trade believe that access may in fact be more limited as trade will commercialize education and consequently escalate the cost of education and perhaps lead to a two-tiered system. Trade is therefore often perceived by critics as a threat to the 'public good' nature of education services, but this requires full and open debate (Newman and Couturier, 2002).

This raises a timely and strategic question regarding the capacity and role of government with respect to providing open or limited access to higher education. For instance, if education is seen as a public function, can private for-profit providers or foreign providers help to fulfil this public function? If so, would foreign for-profit providers be eligible for the same grants, subsidies and tax incentives as public providers under the national treatment obligation of GATS? The prospect of increased trade across borders raises new opportunities and new risks for the question of access to and choice of higher education provision.

Funding

Many of the issues and arguments regarding access can also apply to funding. Some governments have limited budget capacity or lack the political will to allocate funds to meet the needs of higher education. Can international trade provide alternate funding sources or new providers? Trade supporters would answer yes. Or, because of the GATS obligations such as most favoured nation treatment and national treatment obligations, will public funding be spread too thinly across a broader set of domestic and foreign providers? Furthermore, does the presence of foreign providers signal to government that they can decrease public funding for higher and adult education, thereby jeopardizing domestic publicly funded institutions? Does international trade in education advantage some countries, such as those with well-developed capacity for export, and disadvantage others in terms of funding or access? Once again, the impact of more liberalized trade can be a double-edged sword with respect to the funding, either public or private, of higher education teaching–learning and research activities.

Regulation of foreign or cross-border providers

As already noted, the development of a regulatory framework to deal with the diversity of providers and new cross-border delivery modes is needed, and becomes more urgent as international trade increases. In some countries, this will likely mean a broader approach to policy involving licensing, regulating and monitoring both private (profit and non-profit) and foreign providers in order to ensure that national policy objectives are met and public interests protected. It may also involve a shift in government and public thinking towards the view that, while higher education remains a 'public good', both public and private providers can fulfil this public function. This in turn may introduce a competitive edge among providers and general confusion to the consumer. Hence a coherent and comprehensive regulatory framework is called for in order to serve national/domestic interests as well as meeting the needs and protecting the interests of different stakeholder groups, especially the students.

More work is necessary to determine how domestic/national regulatory frameworks are compatible with, or part of, a larger international framework.

Increased connectivity and interdependence among nations, as well as liberalized trade, will mean that more coherence among national frameworks is necessary (Van Damme, 2001). How can coherence between a domestic/national framework and an international framework actually strengthen national regulatory and policy functions rather than weaken them?

Recognition of qualifications

New types of education providers, new delivery modes, new cross-border education initiatives, new levels of student mobility, new opportunities for trade in higher education: all these can spell further confusion for the recognition of qualifications and transfer of academic credits. This is not a new issue. Trade agreements are not responsible for the creation of this scenario of mass confusion, but they contribute to making it more complicated and also to making resolution more urgent. National and international recognition of qualifications and the transfer of credits have already been the subject of a substantial amount of work. The Lisbon Convention on the Recognition of Qualifications of Higher Education in the Europe Region, the European Credit Transfer System and the University Mobility in the Asia-Pacific are good examples of regional initiatives that could lead to the development of a more international approach.

Quality assurance and accreditation

Increased cross-border education delivery and a set of legal rules and obligations in trade agreements require that urgent attention be given to the question of quality assurance and accreditation of education providers (Expert meeting…, 2001). Not only is it important to have domestic/national policy and mechanisms that have the capacity to address accreditation and quality assessment procedures for the academic programmes of new private and foreign providers, it is equally important that attention be given to developing an international approach to quality assurance and accreditation.

There is growing awareness that in the world of cross-border education trade, national quality assurance schemes are being challenged by the complexities of the international education environment. While there may be growing awareness, there is no acceptance or agreement that harmonization of national policies with an international approach to quality assessment and accreditation is needed. No doubt, this opinion will generate heated debate both in support of and against such a development, but it is becoming increasingly clear that while national systems are necessary they are not enough, and perhaps could be more effective if there were greater coherence within an international system. It is imperative that education specialists discuss and determine the appropriate regulating mechanisms at the national and international level and not leave these questions to the designers and arbitrators of trade agreements.

Another potentially contentious issue is the application of quality assurance schemes to both domestic and foreign providers. It may well be that certain GATS conditions, such as the national treatment obligation, require that all providers, domestic and foreign, be subject to the same processes and criteria. In some countries this will not be a problem; in others it will be hotly debated, especially in federations like Canada and Germany.

Quality assurance of higher education in some countries is regulated by the sector, and in others by the government to a greater or lesser degree. The key point is that authority for quality assurance, regulation and accreditation for cross-border delivery needs to be examined and guided by stakeholders and bodies related to the education sector and not left solely in the hands of trade and the market.

Research and intellectual property rights

In the new economy with its emphasis on knowledge production and trade, there is increasingly more value attributed to the creative and intellectual content inherent in both products and services. The Trade-Related Aspects of Intellectual Property Rights (TRIPS) is another trade agreement, completely separate from the GATS, which also addresses trade liberalization. TRIPS covers such things as patents, trademarks and copyright, all of which are salient to the research and teaching–learning functions of the higher education sector. Careful monitoring of TRIPS is also necessary for the higher education sector.

A look at the potential implications of trade agreements on research and scholarly work reveals a number of issues. A consistent theme expressed by trade critics is a deep concern about the increased emphasis on commercialization and commodification of the production of knowledge. Sceptics believe that the highly valued trinity of teaching, research and service of traditional universities may be at risk if a more differentiated and niche-oriented approach to higher education is an outcome of increased trade in education and growing importance of agreements such as GATS and TRIPS.

Internationalization

Attention needs to be given to the impact of trade liberalization on internationalization activities, meaning non-profit or non-trade related international academic activities. Will trade overshadow and dominate the international academic relations of countries and institutions or enhance them (Knight, 1999)? There are many internationalization strategies that can be jeopardized by a purely commercial approach. For example, participation in international development or technical assistance programmes leads to mutual benefits for all partners and has important spinoff effects for research, curriculum development and teaching. Will these programmes have less or more importance when there is increased pressure for trade? Will revenue raised from commercial education activities be used to subsidize internationalization activities? What might happen to student exchange, internships and other forms of academic mobility programmes that do not have an income generation or for-profit motive? Will an institution's limited financial resources be directed to trade initiatives that have an economic return instead of internationalization activities that stress added academic value? How can internationalization and trade activities complement each other? Will bilateral relationships and multilateral networks among institutions shaped by trade opportunities enhance or jeopardize research, curriculum development and other academic endeavours? These are questions that need further discussion and examination. Efforts are needed to profile the benefits and importance of non-profit internationalization and to explore the potential of a mutually beneficial relationship between trade in education and internationalization initiatives.

Mobility of professionals

It has already been noted that GATS is facilitating the mobility of professionals in order to meet the high demand for skilled workers. This affects many of the service sectors and has particular implications for higher education. Not only is higher and adult education responding to the needs of the labour force by providing education and training programmes to meet the market economy, the sector itself is affected by the mobility of its teachers and researchers. In many countries, the increasing shortage of teachers is resulting in active recruitment campaigns across borders. Since many teachers and researchers want to move to countries with more favourable working conditions and salaries, there is a real concern that the most developed countries will benefit from this mobility of education workers at the expense of others.

Culture and acculturation

Last, but certainly not least, is the issue of cultural and indigenous traditions. Education is a process through which cultural assimilation takes place. In fact it is a fundamental vehicle for acculturation. Concern about the homogenization of culture through cross-border supply of higher and adult education is expressed by GATS critics. Advocates maintain that a new hybridization and fusion of culture will evolve through increasing mobility of people and the influence of ICTs. In fact, they believe that this has been happening for decades and is contributing to new cultural exchanges and forms. Once again, the divergence of opinion shows that there are new opportunities and new threats to consider.

Institutional level issues

The emphasis of this section has been on macro policy issues. However the factors affecting individual institutions, especially public higher education institutions, should not be ignored. The foremost issues are institutional autonomy, academic freedom and permanent employment for academic staff (Nunn, 2001b). While these three issues are linked to trade liberalization, they are more closely associated with the larger issues of commercialization and privatization of education, which many believe to be already occurring within borders as well as across borders.

Trade dominates

Finally, it needs to be said that the question of trade liberalization, which most often is interpreted in economic terms, has the potential of dominating the agenda (EI/PSI, 2000). There is a risk of 'trade creep' where education policy issues are being increasingly framed in terms of trade. Even though domestic challenges in education provision are currently on the radar screen of most countries, the issue of international trade in education services will most likely increase in importance. Supporters of freer trade applaud the fact that GATS is seen first and foremost as an economic agreement and that its purpose is to promote and expand free trade for economic reasons. Given that the market potential for trade in higher education is already significant and is predicted to increase, it is clear that GATS and other trade agreements will help to promote trade and further economic benefit. Critics of the trade agreements maintain that the domination of the trade agenda is at the expense of other key objectives and rationales for higher education, such as social, cultural and scientific development and the role of education in promoting democracy and citizenship.

CONCLUDING COMMENTS AND RECOMMENDATIONS

At this stage, it appears that there are more questions than clear answers about the impact and implications of GATS on higher education. The questions are both complex and contentious. They deal with technical/legal issues of the agreement itself; education policy issues such as funding, access, accreditation, quality and intellectual property; and the larger, more political/moral issues for society such as the role and purpose of higher education and whether education is a 'public good' and/or 'tradable commodity'.

This paper ends with a recommendation that education policy makers, researchers and senior administrators give more attention to analysing the opportunities, risks and policy implications emanating from the inclusion of higher education services in GATS and other international trade agreements. The education sector needs to work more closely with trade officials, negotiators and researchers, not only to become better informed of the issues but also to exchange information, provide advice on the implications for education policy and influence future directions of trade of higher education services. Trade officials also need to take the initiative to consult with educators.

It is suggested that international governmental bodies and non-governmental organizations as well as regional and national education groups give more priority to the policy issues emanating from trade liberalization, be proactive in examining how to benefit fully from new opportunities that are available from global competitive trade, and be mindful of risks and unintended consequences. Finally, it is important not to overstate the impact of GATS. Trade in education was alive and well prior to trade agreements. It will undoubtedly increase under the auspices of GATS but policy issues such as funding, access and quality assurance need to be addressed and managed by the education sector and not left to the purview of trade agreements and the WTO.

NOTE

This is an abridged and updated version of a paper 'Trade in Higher Education Services: Implications of GATS', prepared for The Observatory on Borderless Higher Education, March 2002

BIBLIOGRAPHY

Adam, S. 2001. Transnational Education: A Study Prepared for the Confederation of European Union Rectors' Conference. Geneva, Switzerland.

APEC. 2001. *Measures Affecting Trade and Investment in Education Services in the Asia-Pacific Region.* A report to the APEC group on Services 2000.
Singapore, APEC Secretariat.

Arnove, R. and Torres, C. (eds) 1999. Comparative Education: The Dialectic of the Global and the Local. Oxford, Rowman and Littlefield.

Ascher, B. 2001. *Education and Training Services in International Trade Agreements.* Paper presented to Conference on Higher Education and Training in the Global Marketplace: Exporting Issues and Trade Agreements. Washington, D.C.

AUCC. 2001. *Canadian Higher Education and the GATS: AUCC Background Paper.* Ottawa, Association of Universities and Colleges of Canada.

AUCC et al. 2001. *Joint Declaration on Higher Education and the General Agreement on Trade in Services.* Ottawa, Association of Universities and Colleges of Canada, American Council on Education European University Association, Council for Higher Education Accreditation.

Cohen, M. G. 2000. *The World Trade Organization and Post-secondary Education:* Implications for the Public System in Australia. Adelaide, Hawke Institute, University of South Australia. (Working Paper Series, 1.)

Corporate University Xchange. 1999. *Annual Survey of Corporate University Future Directions.* New York, Corporate University Xchange.

Cunningham, S.; Ryan, Y.; Stedman, L.; Tapsall, S. 2000. *The Business of Borderless Education.* Canberra, Department of Education, Training and Youth Affairs.

CVCP. 2000. *The Business of Borderless Education: UK Perspectives.* London, Committee of Vice-Chancellors and Principals.

Davis, D. et al. (eds.) 2000. *Transnational Education: Providers, Partners and Policy. A Research Study.* Brisbane, IDP.

DETYA. 2000. Higher Education Report for the 2000-2002 Triennium. Commonwealth Department of Education, Training and Youth Affairs. ABN:51 452 193 160. Canberra, DETYA.

EI/PSI. 2000. Great Expectations. The Future of Trade in Services. Joint paper published by Education International and Public Services International. Brussels.

——. 1999. The WTO and the Millennium Round: What is at Stake for Public Education. Joint paper published by Education International and Public Services International. Brussels.

Expert Meeting on the Impact of Globalization on Quality Assurance, Accreditation and the Recognition of Qualifications in Higher Education. 2001. Draft Conclusions and Recommendations. Paris, UNESCO.

Foster, A. 2002. Colleges, Fighting US Trade Proposal, Say it Favors For-Profit Distance Education. Chronicle of Higher Education, January 18.

Gottlieb and Pearson. 2001. *GATS Impact on Education in Canada. Legal Opinion.* Ottawa.

Held, D.; McGrew, A.; Goldblatt, D.; Perraton, J. 1999. *Global Transformations: Politics, Economics and Culture.* Cambridge, Polity.

Kelsey, J. 1997. The Globalization of Tertiary Education: Implications of GATS. In: M. Peters Cultural Politics and the University. Palmerston North, New Zealand, Dunmore.

Knight, J. 1999. *A Time of Turbulence and Transformation for Internationalization.* Ottawa, Canadian Bureau for International Education. (Research Monograph, 14.)

——. 2002. Trade in Higher Education Services: The Implications of GATS. United Kingdom. London, The Observatory on Borderless Higher Education.

Knight, J.; de Wit, H. (eds) 1999. Quality and Internationalization in Higher Education. Paris, OECD.

Larsen, K.; Martin, J. P; Morris, R. 2001. *Trade in Educational Services: Trends and Emerging Issues. Working Paper.* Paris, OECD.

NCITE. 2001. Barriers to Trade in Transnational Education. Washington, D.C., National Committee for International Trade in Education.

Newman, K.; Couturier, L. 2002. *Trading Public Good in the Higher Education Market.* Report published by The Observatory on Borderless Higher Education. London.

NUFFIC. 2001. The Global Market for Higher Education: Shifting Roles, Changing Rules. A discussion paper. The Hague, Netherlands Organization for International Cooperation in Higher Education.

Nunn, A. 2001a. *GATS, Higher Education and 'Knowledge Based Restructuring' in the UK*. Research paper. London, UK Association of University Teachers.

———. 2001b. The General Agreement on Trade in Services: An Impact Assessment for Higher Education in the UK. Report. London, UK Association of University Teachers.

MRAT. 2000. New Zealand Exports of Education Services. New Zealand Consortium Working Paper 8. Wellington, New Zealand, Trade and Economic Analysis Division of the Ministry of Foreign Affairs and Trade.

Rui, Y. 2001. China's Entry into the WTO and Higher Education. *International Higher Education*, No. 24 (Summer).

Sauve, P. and Stern, R. (eds). 2000. GATS 2000 New Directions in Trade Liberalization. Washington, D.C., Brookings Institution.

Scholte, J. A. 2000. *Globalization: A Critical Introduction*. London, Macmillan.

Scott, P. 2000. Globalization and Higher Education: Challenges for the Twenty-first Century. Journal of Studies in International Education, Vol 4. No.1.

Sinclair, S. 2000. *GATS: How the WTO's New 'Services' Negotiations Threaten Democracy*. Ottawa. Canadian Centre for Policy Alternatives.

Singh, M. 2001. Re-inserting the 'Public Good' into Higher Education Transformation. In: Kagisano; discussion series published by the Council on Higher Education. South Africa. No. 1, pp. 7–21.

UNESCO Council of Europe. 2001. The UNESCO-CEPES/Council of Europe Code of Good Practice for the Provision of Transnational Education. Paris, UNESCO.

United States Trade Representative. 2000. Submission by the United States to the WTO Council for Trade in Services special session. Washington, D.C.

Van Damme, D. 2001. *Higher Education in the Age of Globalization: The Need for A New Regulatory Framework for Recognition, Quality Assurance and Accreditation*. Working Paper. Paris, UNESCO.

———. 2002. Quality Assurance in an International Environment: National and International Interests and Tensions. Background Paper for the CHEA International Seminar. San Francisco, CHEA.

World Development Movement. 2001. Report of a seminar held by the World Development Movement on the World Trade Organization's General Agreeement on Trade In Services. London, World Development Movement.

WTO. 1998. *Education Services. Background Note by the Secretariat.* Geneva. Council for Trade in Services. (S/C/W/49, 98-3691.)

———. 1999a. The Developmental Impact of Trade Liberalization under GATS. Informal Note by the Secretariat 2748/Rev.1.

———. 1999b. *An Introduction to the GATS.* Geneva, WTO.

———. 1999c. The General Agreement in Trade in Services: Objectives, Coverage, and Disciplines. Prepared by the WTO secretariat. Geneva, WTO.

———. 2000. *Communication from United States: Higher Tertiary. Education, Adult Education and Training.* Geneva, WTO. Council for Trade in Services Special Section. (S/CSS/W/23, 00-5552.)

———. 2001a. Communication from Australia: Negotiating Proposal for Education Services. Council for Trade in Services Special Section. S/SCC/W/110, 01-4716. Geneva, WTO.

———. 2001b. Communication from New Zealand: Negotiating Proposal for Education Services. Council for Trade in Services Special Section. S/CSS/W/93, 01-3215. Geneva, WTO.

———. 2001c. *GATS: Fact and Fiction.* Geneva. WTO.

———. 2002. Communication from Japan: Negotiating Proposal on Education Services. S/CSS/W/137. Geneva, WTO.

Ziguras, C. 2001. *The effect of GATS on Transnational Higher Education: Comparing Experiences of New Zealand, Australia, Singapore and Malaysia.* Paper presented at the Australian Association for Research in Education Annual Conference 2001.

6. Globalization and the Future of Higher Education

Michael Gibbons

I would like to address the topic of globalization and the future of higher education. This is a difficult task, because globalization is so complex a phenomenon that it is difficult to enter into its various processes and extract those likely to have the greatest impact on higher education. The analysis presented here consists, in part, of a detailed consideration of the differences between static and dynamic competition and, because different types of competition imply different types of behaviour, these differences prescribe a range of policies that universities need to put in place to meet the challenge of globalization. Some may find the argument developed in this paper rather abstract, but the intention is to present an analysis that captures just where the dynamics of globalization touch on the operations of universities, the better then to understand what actions to take in response to the new environment.

It may be helpful to make clear at the outset that, though the analysis concentrates on the nature of dynamic competition, it does not represent yet another attempt to cajole universities into behaving more like businesses. Rather the reverse, in fact. Dynamic competition is essential to understanding globalization because it is the process that links globalization to knowledge production and, through that, to one of the main functions that universities perform. Because, in many countries, universities are still the primary, sometimes the only, knowledge-producing institutions, they will inevitably be drawn into the process of dynamic competition, with what consequences for universities we shall have to investigate. While it is certainly a plausible assumption that universities are well placed to play a significant role in that part of the emerging global economy in which dynamic competition elicits 'knowledge solutions', the fundamental question is whether it is possible for them to engage in this form of knowledge production without having to abandon their fundamental values.

The argument of this paper leads to the conclusion that globalization is a driver of change in the university because it is altering the behaviour of academics in the research process itself. There are two elements to this: one involves the emergence of a new set of research practices and the other the spread of research as a recognizably competent activity that is practised beyond the walls of academe.

UNIVERSITIES AND RESEARCH

Let me begin with research by offering, first, a brief description of the range and power of the disciplinary structure as it operates in universities and, second, by laying out what amounts to a new set of research practices that differ in almost every respect from the way research is currently organized and conducted in universities. I will then briefly describe the principal differences between the two sets of research practices in terms of what have been labelled Mode One and Mode Two forms of knowledge production. In a subsequent section of this paper, an explanation is offered about how Mode Two emerges and how it relates to globalization.

The organization of research in universities

The research structures that have gradually been put in place in universities are supported by a set of research practices to ensure that results are sound. These research practices set the rules of the game: that is, the terms of what shall count as a contribution to knowledge, who shall be allowed to participate in its production, and how accreditation shall be organized. Together, these practices underpin what we know as the disciplinary structure of science and scholarship, and this structure, in turn, has come to play a central role in the management and organization of universities today. Of particular importance for what I want to say later is the fact that the disciplinary structure is specialist. Whether in the sciences, social sciences, or humanities, specialism has been seen as a secure way to advance knowledge and its organizational imperatives have everywhere accompanied its adoption.

The disciplinary structure also organizes teaching in universities by providing a framework for the undergraduate curriculum. This structure is the essential link that connects teaching and research, and underpins the argument that in universities they properly belong together. Of course, research not only adds to the stock of specialist knowledge but transforms it as well. The research enterprise is a dynamic one. Its practices articulate the disciplinary structure and, over time, modify what are regarded as the essential ideas, techniques and methods that students need to be taught.

The disciplinary structure, then, has two aspects. In its cognitive aspect, it provides guidelines for researchers about what the important problems are, how they should be tackled, who should tackle them, and what should be regarded as a contribution to the solution. In its social aspect, it prescribes the rules for training and accrediting new researchers, procedures for selecting new university faculty and criteria for their advancement within academic life. In brief, the disciplinary structure defines what shall count as 'good science' and identifies who shall be regarded as 'good scientists'. The disciplinary structure and all that that entails is what I mean by Mode One knowledge production.

Because the disciplinary structure has been institutionalized in them, universities have tended to become the primary legitimators of this form of excellence. But there is a growing amount of evidence to indicate that a new mode of knowledge production may be emerging. In keeping with academic tradition, let us distinguish it from Mode One, and creatively label it as Mode Two. It is the burden of my argument to try to persuade you that the research practices associated with Mode Two are growing up alongside more traditional practices and that they are going to change the shape of universities.

While I am confident that all of you will be familiar with the characteristics of Mode One, the same will probably not be true when it comes to Mode Two. So, let me identify the principal differences between them.

The term Mode One refers to a form of knowledge production – a complex of ideas, methods, values, norms – that has grown up to control the diffusion of the structure of specialization to more and more fields of inquiry, and to ensure their compliance with what is considered sound scientific practice. Mode One is meant to summarize in a single term the cognitive and social norms that must be followed in the production, legitimation and diffusion of knowledge of this kind. For many, research that adheres to these rules is by definition 'scientific' while work that violates them is not. It is partly for these reasons that, whereas in Mode One it is conventional to speak of science and scientists, it has been necessary to use the more general terms knowledge (or research) and practitioners (or researchers) when describing Mode Two. This is intended merely to highlight differences, not to suggest that practitioners of Mode Two are not behaving according to the norms of scientific method. These differences occur right across the research spectrum and can be described in terms of a number of attributes that when taken together have sufficient coherence to suggest the emergence of a new mode of knowledge production.

Analytically, these attributes can be used to allow the differences between Mode One and Mode Two to be specified. Thus:

- In Mode One problems are set and solved in a context governed by the largely academic interests of a specific community. By contrast, in Mode Two knowledge is produced in a context of application.
- Mode One is disciplinary while Mode Two is transdisciplinary.
- Mode One is characterized by relative homogeneity of skills, Mode Two by their heterogeneity.
- In organizational terms, Mode One is hierarchical and, in academic life at least, has tended to preserve its form, while in Mode Two the preference is for flatter hierarchies using organizational structures that are transient.
- In comparison with Mode One, Mode Two is more socially accountable and reflexive.
- Mode One and Mode Two each employ a different type of quality control. Peer review still exists to be sure, but in Mode Two it includes a wider, more temporary and heterogeneous set of practitioners, collaborating on a problem defined in a specific and localized context. As such, in comparison with Mode One, Mode Two involves a much-expanded system of quality control.

Socially distributed knowledge production

The second element that contributes to the evolution of new research practices concerns the spread of research as a recognizably competent activity that is practised well beyond the walls of academe. The past fifty or so years have seen the emergence of a socially distributed knowledge production system. This system comprises a reservoir of skills and expertise that is available for use in a variety of problem contexts and that is now attaining global proportions. In the maintenance of this reservoir, the universities play an important part by providing a supply of trained researchers, as a consequence of which they are now only one player among many in determining the research agenda.

The first thing to note about the emergence of Mode Two is that knowledge production is becoming more complex than it used to be. The key change is that it is becoming less and less a self-contained activity. As practised currently, it is neither the science of the 'universities' nor the 'technology' of industry. It is no longer the preserve of a special type of institution, from which knowledge is expected to spill over or spin-off to the benefit of other sectors. Knowledge production, not only in its theories and models but also in its methods and techniques, has spread from the Academy to many different types of institutions. It is in this sense that knowledge production has become a socially distributed process. At its base lies the expansion of the number of sites that form the sources for a continual combination and recombination of knowledge resources. Metaphorically speaking, what we are seeing is the 'multiplication of the nerve endings of knowledge' and these extend far beyond the boundaries of universities and disciplines housed in them.

Socially distributed knowledge production has five principal characteristics:

- There are an increasing number of places where recognizably competent research is being carried out. This can be easily demonstrated by consulting the addresses of the authors of scientific publications (though change is taking place so rapidly that the full extent of the social distribution of knowledge production is probably no longer fully captured by the printed word).
- These sites communicate with one another and thereby broaden the base of effective interaction. Thus, contributions to the stock of knowledge are derived from an increasing number of tributarial flows from various types of institutions that both contribute to and draw from the stock of knowledge.
- The dynamics of socially distributed knowledge production lie in the flows of knowledge and in the shifting patterns of *connectivity* among these flows. The connections may appear to be random but they move with the problem context rather than according either to disciplinary structures or the dictates of national science policy.
- The number of interconnections is accelerating, so far apparently unchannelled by existing institutional structures, perhaps for the reason that these connections are intended to be functional and to survive only as long as they are useful. The ebb and flow of connections follow the paths of problem interest, and the paths of problem interest are no longer determined by the disciplinary structure of science.

- Knowledge production thus exhibits heterogeneous rather than homogeneous growth. New sites of knowledge production are continually emerging that, in their turn, provide intellectual points of departure for further combinations or configurations of researchers. In this sense, the socially distributed knowledge production system exhibits some of the properties that are often associated with self-organizing systems in which the communication density is increasing rapidly.

In summary, the distributed character of knowledge production constitutes a fundamental change both in the *numbers* of possible sites of expertise and in their degree of *connectivity*. As will become evident, research that draws upon the resources of a socially distributed knowledge system uses different criteria for determining research excellence than those required in discipline-based peer review. To the extent that university researchers operate within the distributed knowledge system, they will import these different types of excellence into the university and hence begin to modify what it is to 'do' good science and scholarship.

GLOBALIZATION, COMPETITION AND INNOVATION

Globalization can be described as the imitation, adaptation and diffusion of technological innovations as the process of industrialization spreads from one country to another. That a particular innovation might undermine, or render obsolete, the basis on which a firm stands, together with the recognition that this threat might arise from an increasing number of places located anywhere in the world, has the immediate effect of increasing competitive behaviour among firms. Further, competition always launches a discovery process and it follows that an increase in competitive behaviour will manifest itself in the intensification of the search for innovations. One way of searching is for firms to engage in R&D activities. It is perhaps because R&D is understood to produce new knowledge that it is frequently argued that, in the process of innovation, knowledge has become the scarce resource. So it might be appropriate to recognize this claim by speaking of innovation as a search for 'knowledge solutions' of various kinds. Globalization, then, describes the spread of industrialization from one country to another. But what is spread are innovations that depend increasingly upon more or less specialized knowledge inputs and this, in turn, is driven by competition between firms.

What is not often enough recognized is that at any given time competition between firms operates simultaneously at two levels: the levels of static and of dynamic competition. The presence of static competition drives a firm to search for efficiency gains by constantly trying to improve the ways in which existing resources are allocated. At this level, the discovery process often involves a degree of R&D activity, sometimes with universities, as firms seek to improve the industrial processes they have adopted and performance characteristics of the products that they currently make. The result is a stream of incremental innovations within the framework of a previously chosen set of technologies; what is often described as a design configuration. At the level of static competition, markets operate to choose among products and, because firms differ in the efficiency with which they operate, there results in each sector a hierarchy of firms distributed around what is sometimes referred to as 'average best practice'.

Under dynamic competition, things are very different. Dynamic competition also launches a discovery process but in a different form, in the sense that it is a search for novel design configurations – novel combinations of scientific ideas and technologies – that might form the bases for the long-term survival of the firm should its existing set of technologies – its current design configuration – be attacked by innovations from one quarter or another. In other words, dynamic competition launches the sort of search behaviour that firms undertake in anticipation of the possibility that from somewhere a knowledge solution will arise that might render their current technological base and associated work force obsolete. But since it is not known what these knowledge solutions will be or where they may arise from, firms deal with this type of risk by participating in joint activities, often joint research activities. To accomplish this, they join networks, enter alliances and form partnerships of various kinds.

In terms of the search process, these collaborations form complex problem-solving sites. Solutions are pursued collaboratively, involving many participants, and, paradoxically, they often involve competitors. Under dynamic competition, markets operate not to choose between products – for there are none yet – but between research groups. And, because groups differ in their creativity, the performance of each research group will depend on its composition. It is, therefore, of the utmost importance for firms which, and how many, research collaborations they join.

Globalization is, in part, about the imitation and adaptation of these 'knowledge solutions' as they diffuse from one firm to another and from one country to another. For the purposes of this exposition, the main point to note is that globalization, because it stimulates dynamic competition, drives the proliferation of collaborative problem-solving sites as it draws more and more firms into its competitive ambit. The evidence for this is unequivocal: the numbers of these collaborative ventures are expanding exponentially across a large number of sectors. Of course, the human resources for these collaborative research ventures are drawn from the employees of firms, but they also make use of the expertise that lies in a socially distributed knowledge production system that is rapidly acquiring a global dimension.

Now, these sites of collaborative research function as 'attractors' for the academic community, in part because in many cases they involve research at the leading edge of a disciplinary field, but also because, for many academics, the opportunity to work in these problem-solving groups provides an important way for them to utilize and develop their specialist skills. If one were to describe some of the principal characteristics of research practice in the search for novel design configurations, it could be said that such research is carried out in the context of application, that it is trans-disciplinary and that it involves heterogeneous sets of skills. Further, one could note that these ventures utilize flatter organizational structures that are, more often than not, transient. Further, to function effectively these forms of collaborative research also need to elaborate broader forms of quality control. As will be evident, this type of collaborative research has many of the characteristics of Mode Two outlined in the section on 'Universities and research'.

In summary, the spread of globalization is accompanied by the prolif-eration of collaborative research arrangements, and these ventures are the sites in which new research practices are being developed. Into this process are drawn an increasing number of members of the academic community. In fact, the numbers of academics participating in this type of industry-driven research are already large enough for the experience to begin to 'feed back' into, and so affect, the ways in which research is pursued in universities. In terms of the description of Mode One and Mode Two research described above, globalization is contributing in no small part to setting up a tension between Mode One and Mode Two research in universities.

Globalization and the universities

This tension manifests itself along many dimensions:

- Among academics: who seek peer recognition for their participation in what is a recognizably different kind of research activity.
- Between academics and the university: for a more differentiated reward structure that recognizes different types of research activity.

- Among universities: in terms of the prestige of having their faculty deemed sufficiently competent to be admitted to these often elite forms of collaborative research.
- Between universities and industry: for sharing of the revenues from intellectual property, which is now more likely to be the outcome not of individual genius but of the joint production of knowledge by experts of many different kinds.

Globalization, through the tensions that it introduces into academic life, is touching the nature of the university at its heart: in the research process itself. It should be noted that, so far at least, the drift of academic researchers into collaborative research with industry has not been the outcome of governmental policy or institutional strategy. The decisions of academics to join these types of collaborative research activities have been largely a matter of individual choice. It is what academics seem to want to do; and, it must be said, it is often an attractive option for the best of them.

If the universities wish to adjust to these changes in the behaviour of their researchers – and it is hard to imagine how they might resist – then they need to modify their recruitment policies, their terms and conditions of work, and their reward structures. But the consequences of such modifications have profound implications for universities as institutions. By becoming so deeply involved in the innovation process, universities are being drawn ineluctably closer to industry. In doing this, or allowing it to happen, they are in fact also changing the basis of their relationship with the wider society. Can universities enter into this new, closer, relationship with industry and still maintain their status as independent, autonomous institutions dedicated to the public good?

The answer must be in the affirmative, but it cannot be accomplished without innovation and change. And the direction of change must not involve the university denigrating the integrity of Mode Two research practices and reaffirming the singular value of discipline-based research practices that are commonly associated with Mode One. Universities do not need to abandon Mode One. Rather, they need to embrace Mode Two more fully. In other words, they need to take their participation in collaborative research beyond the limited business/economic context of the search for novel design configurations. They should not passively support; rather, they should take the lead in facilitating and managing the production of Mode Two research. They need to develop the procedures, organizational forms and reward structures that will produce a type of science (and scientists) that is sensitive to context, that takes the search for knowledge solutions beyond a dialogue of experts and that embraces wider social participation in the research process.

Stated otherwise, and perhaps a little provocatively, the universities, as institutions, need to make a commitment to move from the production of merely reliable knowledge to what might be called the production of socially robust knowledge. At its best, the research practices associated with Mode Two – particularly those that imply wider participation, enhanced social accountability, reflexivity and expanded forms of quality control – can establish an ethos for the production of socially robust knowledge. And it is socially robust knowledge that society is increasingly demanding of its scientific institutions, particularly in the developed world.

CONCLUSION

Somewhat paradoxically, it seems that it is by closer engagement with the wider community in the development and pursuance of research agendas that universities will be able to retain their integrity and impartiality as institutions that serve the public good. It is not by withdrawing into an ivory tower but by entering, more comprehensively and deliberately, the *agora* – those myriad public spaces where issues are discussed and their research implications explored – that universities can move not so much into as 'beyond' the market. It will be through policies of engagement with society, backed up by expertise in the management and production of socially robust knowledge, that universities will be able to remain truly critical participants in the process of globalization. To the extent that universities fulfil this role they will be able to put beyond doubt their status as institutions that, not only in their aspirations but also in their research practices, do indeed serve the public good.

BIBLIOGRAPHY

The ideas presented in this paper are drawn from, and more fully developed in:

Gibbons, M., Limoges, C., Nowotny, H., Schwartzman, S., Scott, P. and Trow, M. 1994. *The New Production of Knowledge: The Dynamics of Science and Research in Contemporary Societies*. London, Sage.

Nowotny, H., Gibbons, M. and Scott, P. 2001. *Re-thinking Science: Knowledge and the Public in an Age of Uncertainty*. Cambridge, Polity.

PART THREE

Universities and Knowledge

7. From Knowledge to Innovation: Remodelling Creative and Knowledge Diffusion Processes

Bernard Pau

I would like to discuss the role of scientific research as it relates to global-ization issues, not only in terms of knowledge acquisition, but also as regards the transmission of this knowledge (through teaching and education) and the challenges of innovation. The chapter will address this topic through a specific example taken from the field of life sciences. To begin with, it is worth noting the fact that the emergence of knowledge in life sciences, particularly during the past decades, has brought to light its integrative dimension – from the microscopic scale to the scale of ecosystems – and the fact that this integrative dimension concerns us, not only as regards the process of the global development of knowledge but also in relation to our role in the world. And it is natural that this reflection on the life sciences and their evolution should lead us to rethink and to reconsider the issue of globalization. The approach that I will adopt in this short essay is thus somewhat symbolic, indeed almost allegorical.

LIFE BEGETS LIFE

Barely a century has passed since Louis Pasteur discovered and then taught us that 'life begets life'. He destroyed the myth of spontaneous generation, causing a complete break, an epistemological revolution, that continues even today: life transmits itself, propagates itself, reproduces itself. Life, therefore, is fundamentally a permanent part of the history of living beings. We know today that life is not reinvented with each generation but rather continues from generation to generation because it is made up of invariants, universal characteristics that give it both its mystery and its strength. I will discuss two or three of these characteristics.

The first is the basic element of a living organism: the cell. Its organization, its spatial domain delimited by its membrane, its metabolisms and physiology give it the very autonomy that makes it the basic element of life. At the same time, this autonomy is accompanied by intense relationships and interactions with its organic tissue environment or its broader environment in the sense of the ecosystem, if we consider, for example, the microbial cell.

Another obviously fundamental universal characteristic of living organisms is the structure and genetic dynamics of the information that makes up the code for the transmission and continuity of life. It is this code, read eternally in the same way, like a sacred oath, that allows an organism to reproduce, creating a virtually exact replica of itself from generation to generation. However, rather than meaning that the living organism is unchanging and constant, this reproduction and continuity pave the way for its diversification. The uncertainty across procreated generations, that is, the uncertainty of the very molecular mechanisms of the reproduction of life, gives rise to biodiversity. Biodiversity, fortunately for us today, is born of uncertainty.

There, then, are a few of the elements of the invariants of living organisms that, far from having been shattered, have been confirmed and deepened during the past twenty years. The spectacular development of technologies for exploring living organisms, both biological and physical, have been accompanied by a tremendous explosion of knowledge. Today, biology is becoming infinitesimally molecular; yet, at the same time, this molecular dissection of living organisms reveals the need for higher meaning. The analytical biomolecular approach provides myriads of information that do not spontaneously form an organized and meaningful body of knowledge but are simply data. There is a pressing need to organize this information into knowledge on a global scale and thus to attain an integrative vision of biology. The best example of this is the analysis of the 'genome'. As you know, the genes of many living organisms, micro-organisms and higher organisms, are today almost completely decoded. However, for the moment this decoding has provided us with few keys to the mysteries of life. Integrative biology, therefore, seeks to visualize the entire functioning of living organisms and thus we no longer talk only about genetics, but about genomics in the sense of a comprehensive and integrated approach to the working of genes.

This is all to say that, no matter how sophisticated our techniques and methods of exploration have become, life is and will always be more than the sum of its molecular or cellular descriptors. Life appears to be more like a kind of superior crystallization that gives meaning to all of this information. Life is an integration: from the cell all the way to planetary ecosystems, everything is linkages, interactions, exchanges of information and meaning. It is communication, many of whose tools are shared by the entire living world. We are perfectly integrated, physiologically integrated, into this world. On that point, the following quotation from one of my favourite poets, Charles Baudelaire, seems particularly illuminating, indeed almost prophetic:

Nature is a temple in which living columns sometimes emit confused words. Man approaches it through forests of symbols, which observe him with familiar glances.

We know today that there are not different living worlds of which we are the spectators, but instead a living universe in which we are the actors and, one might say, its very tissue, and that to observe is therefore also to act.

To summarize the foregoing, albeit using a very bad play on words, from the point of view of the evolution of concepts about living organisms, we cannot but embrace the notion of 'gloBIOlization'. What we are learning from the emergence of biological knowledge today is that there is an integrative globalization of vital phenomenon. We have a fundamentally symbiotic relationship to the world, which essentially implies that even the acquisition of knowledge is not innocent. This acquisition cannot be dissociated from action: it is a distinctive feature of man that tends to modify our relationship to the world and to others. To sum up, this emergent knowledge, this quest for knowledge that is not innocent and thus is consubstantial with our state of 'being in the world', has an ethical and solidarity-based dimension not external to us, but rather a matter of philosophical acceptance.

This idea can be illustrated by a series of observations based on Figure 7.1. A movement of dual integration can be seen today in the field of life sciences and technologies:

Let us first consider vertical integration. Starting from BIOLOGY at the top left of the table, exploratory research in biology – what is still often called 'basic' research – is concerned with developing knowledge; this knowledge is integrated, based on descriptive molecular analysis, into the higher level of integrative organization, which is physiology. This is the

Figure 7.1. Movement of dual integration

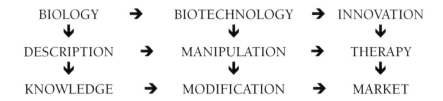

first axis of knowledge integration today. It can no longer be fragmentary; otherwise, it would simply be a set of information. Turning to horizontal integration, the search for knowledge can no longer be isolated from our natural tendency, which is part of our human condition, to modify the living organism. It is in the field of biotechnology that, on the basis of information and knowledge of living organisms, researchers extract and identify elements (proteins, for example) whose changing expression allows us to interpret the emergence of pathologies. As a result of this manipulation of living organisms, which most often consists of modifying genetic material, we can imagine develop new therapies and new drugs. Thus, knowledge, modification, therapy, physiology, innovation and economic development (making these innovative treatments available worldwide) constitute the elements of a two-dimensional integration of humanity's approach to understanding and manipulating living organisms.

AN INTEGRATED AND RESPONSIBLE SYSTEM OF KNOWLEDGE AND INNOVATION

Over the past thirty years, two highly interconnected disciplines, immunology and neuroscience, have given rise to a spectacular leap in knowledge, and it is not unreasonable to expect that within the next twenty years they will lead to even greater integration. For a century, immunology had developed as a descriptive science related to the battle against infection. Today, immunology is much more than that: it is a science dealing with the relationship of humans to the world and themselves. The immune system is the system that defines the immunological self, the foundation of our tissue identity. Thus, today we have an integrated vision of a biological system that defines the self in the context of its relationship to the world. Similarly, in neuroscience, particularly by using the visualization and topographical systems to which physical methods of cerebral imaging give us access, today we are able to make dynamic attributions of functions to cerebral zones. This is a dramatic advance, and it is possible that in the next twenty years we will start to lay the foundations of a theory of the living organism and knowledge, linking biochemical phenomena to the emergence of consciousness and memory.

Thus, broadly speaking, the economy of this system of knowledge and innovation is integrated and responsible. It is here that we find the terms of a truly ethical necessity. An example, which I will not develop here, is the attention that we must give to the creation of drugs that treat or cure some of the serious pathologies that, for reasons of temporary economic myopia, are neglected because a traditional market does not yet exist for them. However, other spaces in the economy of health are conceivable in the near future, including a solidarity-based market.

GLOBALIZATION AS HOMINIZATION

To conclude my modest contribution to this discussion, I have to admit that despite the great clarity of my colleagues' remarks, I find it somewhat difficult to sort out the meanings, or perhaps the very nature, of 'globalization'. When I try to define the term, I find myself facing an uncertainty arising from the multiple usages of the term. Briefly, is globalization a movement that results from our actions or is it our own observation of this movement, which is but one part of our actions and some other interactions? In other words, are we within – as in the movement – or are we without – through observation and finding. As you might imagine, we are both 'within and without', hence our difficulty in understanding it. Perhaps we can agree that, in the generally accepted anthropic sense of the term, for most of us globalization refers to 'globalization of exchange'. If so, it must nevertheless be acknowledged that this globalization of exchange signifies a much deeper and older phenomenon, which appeared at the very moment when humans began to develop knowledge, technology and their actions in the world – in short, when hominids became human. We are now entering a completely new era in our history when, for the first time, humanity is beginning to receive messages back about our very existence on earth. Until now, we have been dealing with an infinite world in which we left our marks without being aware of it. Today, we see reflections of our own actions on earth. Our physical, chemical and even cultural interventions echo our own existence on earth, in the sense that we are not only constituent parts but also powerful modifiers of the earth. From this perspective, like it or not, globalization is above all the age-old and ancestral marks and traces that humankind has left in the world.

Thus, globalization is essentially hominization. Globalization is the hominization of the earth. And if this is the case, at least in part, it means that globalization is neither a concept nor a reality that can be external to us. Inasmuch as it is the result of our action, globalization concerns us both personally and collectively, and in an integrative way. We belong to the very planetary biological tissue that we are modifying.

This development must lead us to take greater responsibility. In one sense, this responsibility is inherent to our desire to survive. The crucial question we must ask ourselves is: Is humankind truly important – must humanity survive? Our species shoulders a great responsibility in the response to this question. And this responsibility also has organizational, logistical and cultural meanings, because every system of exchange (if globalization is to be taken as exchange), whether political, economic, financial or cultural, fundamentally reduces the dimensions of our existence in the world. We experience this every day in the constraints imposed by an exchange system that simplifies the incredible richness of our relationship to the world and to others. This richness, though obviously multidimensional, is becoming unidimensional, as if being projected over the surface of the earth. Thus, our responsibility is perhaps to foster the resurgence of all these dimensions, or in any case to give priority to the third dimension of exchange, which I think should be called solidarity. Solidarity with the world around us and with others is a way to give substance to the path we are pursuing.

KNOWLEDGE AND SOLIDARITY

There are probably two key areas where this solidarity must be expressed in an urgent and determined way in the new century. One relates to the field of energetics (which I will not discuss here) and the other to the field of knowledge. We are entering the century, or the millennium, of the knowledge-based economy; knowledge is therefore a major area in which we must exercise our responsibility of solidarity. Thus, since it is better to share knowledge and a good philosophy is one that we can apply, I enthusiastically embrace John Daniel's proposal: 'Let ... universities commit themselves to the notion of knowledge as a public good and make their learning materials freely available on the Web.' One of our responsibilities, based on the science that generates knowledge, is to deliver knowledge and to deliver as much as possible of it immediately and without constraints. From such knowledge will emerge a new shared meaning of the multiplicity of relationships to the world, a meaning that is essential to the building of peace and development.

For our purposes, and as the 'practical and experimental work' of this philosophy, at Montpellier we have developed 100 hours of global and integrated teaching in biotechnology for French students. Its purpose is to allow students to achieve a certain level of performance in the disciplines and methods of modifying the living organism. This summer, I began to propose that this mediatized teaching (on the Internet and video) be made available, free of charge, to countries that want to use it to accelerate their access to and appropriation of these technologies. Discussions regarding this are currently under way with Lebanon and Tunisia.

I want to emphasize the urgency of the need to share knowledge, and to organize ourselves to do this without delay. It is an essential condition of what our own development holds in store for us: a true renaissance.

8. The Global Knowledge Wall

Riccardo Petrella

CHALLENGES FOR UNIVERSITIES

Development is a major challenge for universities. It speaks to the scientific basis of university teaching. As a notion applied to society, development has become part of the scientific and political language of the western world since the Second World War. But how can academia talk about 'human development', 'economic development' and 'social development' when it is recognized in all quarters that social, economic and human inequalities have only become more widespread and deeper, particularly during the past twenty years? Moreover, why have we been talking about the need to promote 'sustainable development' since the 1970s, thus inferring that the development achieved until now has not been 'sustainable' from the environmental, socio-economic and human perspectives?

This major challenge gives rise to three other key issues that universities will now have to deal with. There is first the need for scientific rigour in the knowledge produced by our universities. The production of knowledge is increasingly influenced by extra-scientific imperatives, particularly those related to the interests of persons with military and economic/financial power. The second issue concerns the ethical responsibility of academics. In the face of the non-sustainability of current development and of the system that shapes it (the capitalist market economy), can academics continue to invoke the supposed neutrality of science? Can they go along with the mythology that suggests that constructive criticism of the dominant system is permitted but more forceful criticism would be tantamount to the gratuitous demonization of the capitalist market economy? The third issue relates to the very function of the university. Can the university live with being the basis for the legitimation of a new 'human divide': the 'knowledge divide'?

These then are the points for consideration and debate on which I will concentrate during this necessarily brief presentation. Of course, I will conclude with a series of proposals. Criticism is essential and fundamental. Any scientific, but also political (socially aware), undertaking is a mixture of the accumulation and acceptance of the knowledge produced elsewhere and before us as well as the questioning and challenging of this very same knowledge. However, this is not sufficient, particularly at the political, social, economic and cultural levels. We must constantly strive to formulate proposals aimed at promoting new and alternative developments, situations and solutions.

DEVELOPMENT IN CRISIS:
A CONCEPTION OF THE WORLD AND SOCIETY

The notion of development theorized, imposed and practised throughout the world since the Second World War has been based on an essentially economic and techno-deterministic conception of the growth of production, consumption and income in monetary and financial terms. It is no longer a secret to anyone, even if political leaders as powerful as the current President of the United States appear to be unaware of it, that this notion of development has been in a state of crisis since the mid-1970s.

By the late 1960s and early 1970s, several factors obliged the world of the powerful, including the academic world, to talk more first about 'human development', as opposed to materialistic economic development dominated by technology and finance, and then about 'sustainable development'. These factors include: the saturation of the economies of Western countries; the break-up of the international financial system established after the Second World War and replaced by a structurally unstable system left to speculative forces; the increase in structural unemployment from the 1970s onwards; the explosion of environmental spills and disasters along with the crises of cities and the growth of daily violence, not to mention the resurgence, beginning in the 1980s, of increasingly profound social and economic inequalities between countries and social groups within countries.

Therefore, the past twenty years have been marked by a worsening of the human condition in the world, with the exception – if one judges by certain criteria of wealth and comfort – of a minority of the world population. An obvious question emerges from this recent history: Can universities continue to invest hundreds of millions of euros annually, at the global level, in teaching and research on 'sustainable development' and just 'development' without denouncing the true negative, insufficient and deceptive impact of actual 'development' and without searching for solid and valid alternative solutions?

It is increasingly difficult for the large segments of the populations that are excluded from world wealth – 2.7 billion people live in poverty at the moment – to accept that a large proportion of university researchers and professors continue to provide so-called scientific evidence, as was the case at the recent Johannesburg Summit, in support of theses advanced by established interests. These interests are being defended by large multinational companies in the chemical, petroleum, pharmaceutical, automobile, water, computer, construction, telecommunications and agri-business industries; by the military apparatuses of the United States and other Western European powers as well as those of India, China and the Russian Federation; and, finally, by the very powerful elites in the countries of the North.

Similarly, we must ask why the majority of academics who are in favour of Genetically Modified Organisms (GMO) and Intellectual Property Law in the field of living organisms are linked by research funding and other factors to large private pharmaceutical, chemical and agri-food companies. Another example is that most of the academics who openly support the idea of water being treated as an economic good and the refusal by political leaders in the Western world to recognize access to water as a right are 'experts' working for or in connection with large international water companies such as Vivendi Environment, Suez Ondeo, RWE–Thames Water, United Water, Bechtel, Nestlé, Danone, Coca-Cola, Hydro-Quebec and the now-defunct Enron Corporation. All of these companies were amply represented at the Second World Water Forum in The Hague in March 2000 and at the Johannesburg Summit in September 2002.

Finally, major ethical questions should also be raised about the current dominant attempt within universities in the Western world to reduce economics to a denuded, aseptic, theoretical approach based on the so-called 'value-free' quantification and modelling taught in MBA programmes. A recent striking example of this trend comes from Germany where the federal government has given its political and 'moral' support to the creation, by a dozen large, private German companies, of a European Business School in Berlin. The purpose of this new university is ultimately to compete with the major MBA schools of Fontainebleau (INSEAD), Barcelona (IMED), Lausanne (IMD) and Harvard (Harvard Business School) although, until recently, Germany was still resistant to the MBA culture. Such a trend shows that universities are far from clearly and rigorously adopting critical positions on current 'development' processes, such as the so-called 'human' or 'sustainable' development. Rather they are increasingly participating in the promotion of education or training about a development that is centred on private enterprise and the logic of maximizing the appreciation of financial capital and, more specifically, the competitive capacities of conquest and survival of private multinational companies on world markets for the purpose of maximizing capital efficiency.

In this situation, what is the true meaning of 'scientific' knowledge as it relates to the fundamental question of 'development'? In other words, development for whom, by whom, how and under what conditions?

REQUIREMENT FOR SCIENTIFIC RIGOUR IN KNOWLEDGE PRODUCTION

Scientific rigour is a vital requirement in all fields of knowledge that are closely related to the living world. This is especially the case with the life of human beings (biology, health, information, communication, energy, economics, law, ecology, etc.) because knowledge has increased the ability of human beings to intervene in all living phenomena. This leap in human power can lead to many excesses, which are already verifiable. Scientists cannot be left to control their own power through their voluntary ethical codes, as the experience of voluntary codes of conduct of companies abundantly demonstrates.

In my opinion, greater scientific rigour is urgently needed, especially in three areas. The first concerns the definition, promotion and 'management' of life and the rights of and to life. The requirement of scientific rigour is found here in the different forms of promotion and management that are expressed in the attacks and assaults on the rights of and to life for everyone, as well as by the merchandizing of life, and the appropriation and control of life by private subjects. For example, economic euthanasia, the patentability of living organisms and the privatization of health care services are all claimed to be essential to living in dignity. These are just some of the subjects for which the various scientific disciplines should guarantee greater scientific rigour, if only through a real and truly effective transdisciplinarity and a greater responsibility of academics toward the community and future generations, notably through the application, among other things, of the precautionary principle.

Second, there is the very subject of globalization. The predominant theories in this field today are based on theses that do not respect any criteria of scientific validity, like the theses on historical 'naturality' and thus the 'inevitability' of the current forms and content of economic and financial globalization of Western economies. The theoretical and political confusions surrounding the debates over globalization do not reflect the diversity of the situations and phenomena taken into account – which would be normal and understandable – but mainly the weakness of the theoretical foundations and scientific approaches due to an academia that has become very susceptible to the demands and ideas of the dominant political and economic world. This academia very often thinks, either for convenience or from conviction, that a critical position cannot be taken regarding current globalization, and considers that the only possible reasonable option is humanization and a better 'social regulation' of current globalization. The same is true of theses about the coming of the information and communication society, considered by the powerful to be the flip side, with globalization, of the same new society that has been created during the past thirty years. Like theses on the inevitability of globalization, those on the information society are also scientifically weak. They express the rhetoric of a world-conquering class that is seeking in this way to legitimize its plans and dreams to expand its power throughout the world. The fact that the majority of academics are willing to support and justify such plans and dreams should be of concern to us and give us the incentive to take greater responsibility.

My third and final area concerns all the concepts and realities related to humanity, the global community, the global society, globality, world common goods, world law and, through them, the notions and phenomena of sovereignty (which, of whom, how?), security (of whom, which, by whom?), world political representation and global government (and not this great academic and political deception passing itself off as 'governance'), world public services, the redistributive tax system and relations between the local and the global. In this field, scientists are beginning a great adventure in the realm of knowledge. However, to delay now would be dangerous. The slogans – and they are short-term, invented and marketed by Western and westernized gurus to serve the powerful – cannot replace the theses that depend on the solid work of theoretical and empirical validation. Fortunately, they do not have to start from square one. From China to India, Africa and the Arab world, from Greece and Rome to the Amerindians and Kant, we have amassed a great storehouse of knowledge and experience.

FACING THE NON-SUSTAINABILITY
OF 'CURRENT DEVELOPMENT'

Fortunately, during the past fifty years, a very small number of academics have, along with others, represented the civil conscience of our societies by denouncing the negative effects of the development of the chemical industry on human health, and in particular on work. They have also raised the alarm and kept us aware of major technological hazards. It is obvious that on the economic, social, environmental and cultural levels, the non-sustainability of the current economy would have been much worse if it were not for this ever active, critical and opposing minority. Not only are they struggling to denounce the wrongdoings of a society which is increasingly dominated by a mercantilist and highly productivist logic that serves the interests of private financial capital, but also to propose other priorities for science and technology and different applications of this very same science and technology.

This struggle has now taken on even greater urgency. Academics must therefore exercise their responsibility in a forceful, clear and uncompromising manner in three particular areas: war, violence, and injustice.

War has always divided academics. Today, this is all the more true given the declaration by the world hegemonic superpower that a total, global and preventive just war against so-called global terrorism is unavoidable. It seems to me that the academic world's resistance or opposition to this war is not as strong and determined as it should be. We realize that to make people embark on the course of a long, global, total war implies a spectacular rise in large budgets for leading-edge research in all fields. However, such a windfall cannot in any case justify the half-hearted resistance or opposition of academics.

The violence inherent in the liberalized, deregulated, privatized and competitive capitalist market economy structurally affects small and medium-sized businesses, small shopkeepers and small farmers who are continuously swept aside in developed countries. There is also the violence against unprofitable workers or human resources and against small shareholders. The fragile pensions of such shareholders are a Sword of Damocles fuelling feelings of insecurity widespread among people of modest means. There is the violence against those of whom only the strongest and most competitive are promised wealth and power; against the global environment, which continues to suffer according to data presented at the Johannesburg Summit; against minority cultures whose future would only be guaranteed if they succeeded in becoming merchandise and an integral part of the most solvent and lucrative world trade.

Academics who attended the Johannesburg Summit should not have endorsed the final documents approved by the Summit because of issues of injustice. In Johannesburg, it was formally and widely accepted that injustice is inevitable. Academics who were at the Summit should have left it as soon as it became clear that the Summit officials (including the United Nations Secretary-General), supported by the more powerful states, had decided to conclude with the affirmation that the maximum goal the Summit could set for itself should be to halve the number of people living in poverty by 2015. This goal had already been affirmed at the Millennium Summit in New York in September 2000 and reiterated at the International Conference on Financing for Development in Monterrey in March 2002.

Nevertheless, since it was specified in the final political declaration of the Johannesburg Summit that the number of poor people used as a basic reference – 1.3 billion – is the number of people who 'live' on less than $1 a day, this means that the world leaders have accepted an ambitious goal of 3 billion and 50 million poor people in 2015. The calculation is simple. According to UN statistics, there are currently 2.7 billion poor people (those whose income is less than $2 a day) of whom 1.3 billion are extremely poor people who live on less than $1 a day. Halving the 1.3 billion of extremely poor people means that it is acknowledged that there will still be 650 million extremely poor people in 2015, in addition to the 1.4 billion poor people with less than $2 a day, totalling 2 billion and 50 million. The current increase in population – 80 million new inhabitants per year – must be added to this total, in other words, an additional 1.2 billion people (80 million × 15 years). Since all these new inhabitants will be born among the poor in Asia, Africa, Latin America, and assuming that 200 million of them will be relatively rich, it must be estimated that there will be an additional 1 billion poor people in 2015, that is, a total of 3 billion and 50 million poor people. We are living with the most glaring human and social injustice, and no academic should support such a destiny.

UNIVERSITIES AND THE KNOWLEDGE DIVIDE

By knowledge divide, we mean the gap between those who produce and control the use of knowledge 'that matters' and those who are excluded from it or are incapable of adopting the means to produce it and/or control its applications. The knowledge divide is linked with the theories that were fashionable in the United States in the 1980s on the emergence of a knowledge-driven economy and, as a result, supposedly also of a knowledge-based society. These theories subsequently became the new 'Bible' of UNESCO and the OECD. The European Union, for its part, also adopted them as its new credo following that of competitiveness (prevailing from the 1980s onwards) and of socio-liberal globalization (prevailing in the 1990s). Currently, nearly all the political and economic leaders of the European Union countries firmly believe, with the assistance of academics, in the triple paradigm of competitiveness, globalization and the knowledge economy. According to theories of the knowledge-driven economy and the knowledge-based society developed by academics in our universities, knowledge has become the principal source of wealth creation. Knowledge represents the basic capital, the most precious economic good, whose right of ownership should be ensured, guaranteed and protected. Hence the importance acquired by the Intellectual Property Law and the corresponding organization, the World Intellectual Property Organization (WIPO).

Our societies tend to reduce the notion of knowledge to 'that which matters' to the capitalist market economy: physics, chemistry, biology, mathematics, computer science, management and marketing. Thus, the value of knowledge is defined on the knowledge market, which is currently represented by cyberspace – the Internet. According to theories of the knowledge society, the network (the Web) is an infinite, boundaryless knowledge market that is open to all those who are familiar with the language of knowledge that matters. Thus, the knowledge divide is not – according to the predominant views – the result of a structural dysfunctioning of the current system related to the unequal and excluding logic that is specific to the system, but is due to the fact that those who are excluded or marginalized fail to value or do not sufficiently value the accessibility to the market of training, education and information offered by the system to all who start out on an equal footing. In other words, the knowledge divide reflects the inequalities that are regarded as normal and inevitable between individuals. Academics can hardly support such a myth.

FOR A COMMITMENT IN FAVOUR
OF A NEW 'NARRATIVE OF THE WORLD'

Decidedly internationalist and open to an integrated vision of life and the world, universities must commit themselves to a new narrative of human society over the next twenty years. This new narrative should be based on the following three proposals.

- Primacy of knowledge in the service of the right to live with dignity for all human beings and for all the 8 billion people who will live on the planet in the year 2020. This means that all our sciences and technologies must be developed so that everybody will have access to safe drinking water (and sanitation), basic food, clean housing, health, education and information by the year 2020.
- Recognition of knowledge as a common good of humanity. Thus, it is advisable to amend radically the principles related to the Intellectual Property Law, and within this framework redefine the scopes and limits of Copyright Royalties, Trade Rights and Industrial Rights. Current patents are legalized acts of piracy perpetrated on the products of the earth, life and the common goods of humanity. In this respect, the initiative taken by MIT to release its distance education from the constraints of Intellectual Property Rights should be positively welcomed. Similarly, the free software movement should be supported.
- Imposition of structural limits on the exploitation of planetary resources. Sustainable development must not involve producing and consuming more at a lesser cost but exploiting and consuming less. Concepts such as frugality, slowness and sharing for a better life must prevail over those of productivity, growth, speed, private appropriation and competitiveness.

It is not easy to put into practice these three founding proposals: the right to life for everyone, promotion of world common goods and the quest for wisdom. Neither is it impossible. Universities have sufficient tools and means – and, especially, the power of their students' dreams, desires and enthusiasm – to undertake such an adventure. Students are not there to be trained to become the new conquerors of the world, but rather to learn how to become citizens, like everybody else, and to live in synergy with respect for previous generations (to the extent necessary) as well as for the future generations' right to live with dignity. If universities are not prepared to teach this, then it should not be surprising that injustice, violence and war will remain the typical forms of behaviour of human beings.

PART FOUR

Globalization, Universities and Development

9. Mastering Globalization: From Ideas to Action on Higher Education Reform

David E. Bloom

Almost everyone sees *education* as essential to development, but until recently very few of those responsible for formulating education policy for the developing world have acknowledged the value of *higher* education. Organizations like the World Bank have traditionally accorded higher education a relatively low priority, believing both that it favoured the elite in society and that returns on higher education investment were much lower than returns on investment in primary and secondary education. In its new report, *Constructing Knowledge Societies: New Challenges for Tertiary Education*, the Bank itself has admitted that: 'Much of the support provided by World Bank tertiary education projects was piecemeal… The Bank was rarely able to offer the type of long-term comprehensive support for tertiary education that is required for successful reform and effective institution building'.

Globalization is exposing this position – where on the one hand education is said to be essential, and on the other the most advanced type of education is neglected – as being fundamentally inappropriate to developing countries' needs. The process of globalization is making higher education more important than ever before, and the neglect of this sector seriously threatens development.

As this paper will argue, globalization exerts new pressures on higher education, making reform essential. But ideas on reform are not enough, and herein lies another contradiction relating to both development and higher education: the policy community devises many possible reforms, but does little to promote effective implementation. This, of course, applies to most development priority areas, but this paper will focus on three main points, all related to higher education.

- Higher education is essential to promoting sustainable human development and economic growth. It is no longer a luxury that only rich countries can afford, but an absolute necessity for all countries, and especially for poor ones.
- The pressures of globalization make it urgent that we devote substantially more resources to the tertiary education sector, and that we also reform it at both the level of individual institutions and the system as a whole.
- Good ideas are not enough; focusing on implementation is at least as important as policy design. The harsh realities of taking an idea to the field and bringing it to scale must be considered in the design of policy.

THE IMPORTANCE OF HIGHER EDUCATION

Globalization has turned a piercing spotlight onto each country's higher education systems and institutions. Globalization refers to the process whereby countries become more integrated via movements of goods, capital, labour and ideas. Trade (the main channel through which this is occurring) offers great advantages because it allows each country to specialize in what it does best – in other words, to have a more refined international division of labour. Globalization has both facilitated and been facilitated by advances in information and communications technology. These advances, coupled with the increasingly refined international division of labour, have meant that new ideas are quickly brought to fruition and new technologies developed, and superseded, more rapidly than at any other time in history. Knowledge has become an increasingly important determinant of the wealth of nations, and access to knowledge, together with the ability to disseminate it, has become a major source of competitive advantage.

Higher education can be a vital tool for helping developing countries to benefit from globalization. So far, most technological advances have been born in the developed world. Although rich countries are home to just 15 per cent of the world's population, they are responsible for over 90 per cent of patents granted.[1] If developing countries aspire to catch up, higher education can be a fundamental instrument for speeding that process. Learning how to access ideas and technologies developed elsewhere and put them into practice – skills that higher education is uniquely well suited to build – can enable developing countries to garner the benefits of globalization without the laborious and costly process of discovery. Higher education can also help countries attract foreign investment and participate more effectively in international affairs, given the technical demands of diplomacy, international commerce and global governance. In other words, higher education can help developing countries use the economic transformation being wrought by globalization to leapfrog stages of development.

Globalization, in turn, can help a country benefit from the products of higher education. One of the problems in the Arab world is that, in countries such as Egypt and Jordan, many young people are emerging from higher education institutions with no jobs to fill. Rigid labour markets and a failure to connect to global trade routes have led to relative isolation and economic stagnation in much of the Middle East. Having large numbers of well-educated but unemployed young people can be a recipe for unrest. Well-managed integration into the global economy, on the other hand, can boost economies, promote foreign investment and create jobs, enabling countries to take advantage of the products of their higher education systems and benefit from their skills and knowledge. Globalization can also help institutions benefit from lessons learned in other countries, and from linking up with foreign institutions to solve problems.

The combination of globalization and higher education offers huge potential for improving living standards. India, for example has taken advantage of globalization by building up its software engineering industry, in terms of trained software engineers, back office services industry, and new companies and projects. The economies of those parts of India such as Bangalore and Hyderabad that are participating in these activities are flourishing, and provide a good example of a country using higher education to take advantage of one of the many promising opportunities offered by globalization. Over 80,000 people work in Bangalore's high-tech industry, many of them products of the city's 100 research universities and technical colleges. IBM, Intel, Microsoft, Oracle and Sun Microsystems have all either set up software development centres or established links with local firms so that they can take advantage of India's supply of well-trained computer graduates.

But the international community, and most developing countries themselves, have yet to realize the enormous benefits of higher education. Large gains have been made in promoting basic and secondary education, but the UN's Millennium Development Goals, and the recent declaration of the World Summit on Sustainable Development in Johannesburg, make no mention of tertiary schooling.

It is particularly striking that higher education is not mentioned as an instrument for achieving even one of the eight Millennium Development Goals of the United Nations (see p.235 for a list of these goals). Yet attainment of every single one of them will be much easier if a country has a strong and productive higher education system.

The first two goals, for example – halving the proportion of people whose income is less than a dollar a day and the proportion living in hunger by 2015 – are largely reliant on economic development and poverty reduction measures. Without a higher education system, who is going to devise poverty reduction strategies? Who is going to carry out the agricultural research to develop the technologies appropriate for those living off the land? And who is going to put in place policies that promote economic development and negotiate debt relief and access to rich-world markets at the WTO?

The next goal – ensuring universal primary education – is also reliant on higher education to train the teachers who will ensure that increased quantity of education is matched by improved quality.

And this also applies to most of the other six goals. Empowering women requires, among many other things, women who have the skills to hold positions of power. Reducing infant mortality requires better-trained medical staff. And reversing the loss of environmental resources needs, among many other knowledge-driven initiatives, research into alternative energy sources. All are also closely linked to educational achievement, and particularly the skills in knowledge development and application that higher education produces.

The point is that higher education offers great opportunities for developing countries to benefit from, and help direct, the process of globalization. It can contribute to achieving the Millennium Development Goals, and it can empower countries to adopt new technology to meet domestic needs and help them catch up with the global economy.

Unfortunately, this need for higher education in developing countries is going largely unmet. In much of the developing world, higher education delivery is woefully unsuited to the demands of globalization. Existing systems satisfy neither the requirements of the global labour market nor domestic social and economic needs. Issues needing attention include the following:

- Where today's world requires problem-solving skills and flexibility, many of today's developing country universities focus on rote learning, where memory rather than creativity and curiosity is rewarded. In a fast-changing world, higher education institutions must teach their students not only what is known now, but also how to keep their knowledge up to date. Flexibility and a grasp of new knowledge-gathering technologies are vital, but sadly lacking in most of the developing world.

- Equally important is the failure of curricula to encompass the knowledge, skills and perspectives students need to know. As the recent Task Force on Higher Education and Society stated (see below for more on their report), infrastructure constraints and a reliance on tradition have left many arts and humanities graduates ensconced in the ranks of 'educated unemployment'.

- Higher education systems are failing to take advantage of opportunities offered by global integration. Globalization is allowing people to burrow out of the confines of their own institutions and link up with others to solve problems, but cross-institutional and cross-border networks, which offer great promise for promoting scientific innovation appropriate to developing countries' needs, are as yet few and far between.

THE NEED FOR REFORM

The need for reform was the focus of the report of the Task Force on Higher Education and Society, which was co-convened by UNESCO and the World Bank in 1997 and whose report was issued in 2000.[2] The Task Force suggested that 'urgent action to expand the quantity and improve the quality of higher education in developing countries should be a top development priority'. Higher education, the report states, 'is to a knowledge economy as primary education is to an agrarian economy and secondary education is to an industrial economy'.

The Task Force report was something of a landmark in higher education thinking. World Bank President James Wolfensohn described it as a 'wonderful road map' for development policy-makers. 'Well-educated people from the developing world', he said in launching the report, 'can be a powerful force for change, but they need schools and academic opportunities in their own countries.' The report outlines the case for higher education reform, addresses the obstacles, and suggests ways of overcoming them. The following is a brief summary of the report's five interrelated themes.

Higher education and the public interest

Modern ignorance about higher education has been led by economists, who have had an overly simple way of assessing the return on investments in higher education. The basic problem is that they have measured the return on education exclusively through wage differentials. With reference to someone who has no education, someone who has been to primary school, someone who has completed secondary school and someone with a university degree, one can ask how much more each earns. These differences are then compared to the incremental amounts invested in their education to find the return. The results generally suggest that higher education yields a lower return than primary or secondary education, and they have been used to justify the skewing of government budgets (and development funds) away from higher education institutions.

The rate-of-return calculations are flawed at the very least because they do not take account of the full range of benefits to those who receive higher education. For example, higher education can enhance health and reduce fertility, so the private benefits to the individual are not just the direct labour productivity benefits that the rate-of-return analysis suggests.

Looking more broadly, however, higher education *obviously* confers benefits above and beyond enhancing the incomes of those who receive their degrees. And many of these benefits take the form of public goods, such as the contribution of higher education to enterprise, leadership, governance, culture and participatory democracy, and its potential for lifting the disadvantaged out of poverty. These are all vital building blocks for stronger economies and societies, and all routes by which the benefit of investment in higher education multiplies throughout society.

Systems of higher education

Improving higher education requires the adoption of a system wide perspective on higher education, that is, viewing the structure and operation of higher education institutions in concert, not just individually. A higher education system encompasses everything from public research universities to private vocational schools. A system wide perspective will need to address the place of these institutions *vis-à-vis* each other, as well as their links to the rest of the education system and the broader society. Such a perspective lends itself naturally to the development of a rational and stratified system of higher education *in the public interest*, with different types of institutions, from research universities to vocational colleges, dedicated to different missions. Links to higher education institutions in other countries are also becoming increasingly important.

Governance
In the view of many people involved with higher education in the developing world, governance – the arrangements, both formal and informal, that allow the higher education 'team' to function – is *the* key problem impeding the effectiveness of higher education institutions. A set of principles – such as academic freedom, autonomy, the need for monitoring and accountability, and meritocratic selection – is essential in beginning to address this problem. Tools for converting these principles into action, ranging from specific mechanisms for hiring and promoting faculty and appointing university administrators, to boards of trustees, faculty councils, institutional handbooks and visiting committees, are also critical.

Science and technology
Science and technology present a unique set of challenges for universities across the world. First, basic science is itself a public good. Basic scientific inquiry often needs huge investment to deliver long-term but highly uncertain benefits. The market is not very good at funding this research on its own, especially when the benefits will be felt by the poor more than the rich. Researching a cure for malaria, for example, has had low priority.

Second, the way that scientific knowledge is produced is changing rapidly. Increasingly, science is carried out across organizational and disciplinary boundaries, involves public and private sector participation, and is often directed toward working in teams to solve a strategically important problem, such as developing an HIV/AIDS vaccine, rather than having individual scientists working alone in a relatively uncoordinated manner in their laboratories.

Third, scientific progress is leading to growing uncertainty, rather than certainty. The furore over genetically-modified foods – which ties together cutting-edge science, big business and globalization – is a perfect example of how difficult it has become to understand where a particular scientific advance is taking us.

These three factors mean that universities must be substantially more flexible if they are to fund science adequately, pull together the highest calibre of scientific teams, build curricula relevant to modern societies and maintain public support for their scientific research.

These problems are compounded in many developing countries, where, due to weak human resources, inadequate equipment, a lack of connectivity to the rest of the research world and many other factors, the science and technology base is currently low. Developing such a base is no longer optional, but is becoming mandatory for all countries trying to compete in the global knowledge economy.

The importance of general education

General education emphasizes the development of the whole individual, and not just occupational training. It highlights the ability to think, communicate and learn and to adopt a broad historical, comparative and disciplinary perspective on different issues. It is also a foundation for later, more specialized, study.

Developing countries could benefit from the introduction – or in a few cases the expansion – of high-quality general education. Such an education is not for all students, but it is in each country's public interest to have individuals who can operate at a high intellectual level in rapidly changing times – whether that involves negotiating with the International Monetary Fund, deciding whether to import generic AIDS drugs, deliberating on the ethical issues surrounding genetically modified food, or acting to develop a national legal system that can robustly protect fundamental human rights.

The content of general education curricula will naturally vary across countries. For example, South Africa should not blindly adopt a Canadian model. Rather, it should take lessons learned elsewhere and adapt them to the needs of South African society. Similarly South Africa, where English is widely spoken, may not need the same language courses as a country such as the Republic of Korea. It may, however, need more courses in building strong institutions, so individuals educated in subjects like law, philosophy, economics and politics might be relatively more important. Designing a general education programme offers the opportunity to ask fundamental questions about what matters to a particular society. It offers the opportunity to focus on a country's history, its culture and its values. Doing this will help energize the whole higher education system and, in time, change the way a society thinks about itself, too.

IMPLEMENTATION

Good ideas by themselves are simply not enough. The field of international development is littered with sensible policy suggestions that have come to nothing in practice. As noted earlier, there is a contradiction here – in both the development arena as a whole and higher education in particular – where much more time is spent discussing policy design than how the policy is actually going to be implemented.

Two issues – curriculum reform and brain drain – illustrate some of the difficulties in implementing new higher education policies in the era of globalization.

Curriculum reform is widely recognized as being necessary if higher education institutions in developing countries are to produce graduates capable of participating and competing in our emerging global society. But curriculum reform is usually seen as purely a technical problem, as distinct from a political one. In fact it is both a technical and a political problem, and the failure to recognize the political aspects of curriculum reform is usually the cause of its undoing.

In many cases, the failure of reform can be ascribed to the adoption of a top-down committee approach. Stakeholder involvement is vital to curriculum design and reform, and leaving out interested and affected parties can be fatal. All parties with an interest in reform (including teachers, students, administrators, employers and donors) must be encouraged to voice their views. Current faculty in particular must be handled with care, as they are often the ones who feel most threatened by curriculum change. Without this widespread involvement, reformers will fail to bring on board the very people responsible for curriculum delivery.

The political obstacles to reform are also highlighted by the brain drain issue. Highly trained human resources can be bought, and they can be bought more easily now because there is more mobility. Students who are skilled in the development and acquisition of knowledge are tempting targets for firms wishing to get an edge over their competition and for governments and international development organizations needing to fill vacant posts. This has led to brain drain, where students whose education has been paid for by a developing-world government remain (or go) abroad with the skills they have acquired, and thereafter contribute little but remittances to their home country.

Brain drain makes it difficult to argue the case for investment in higher education. If a sizable number of a country's best students, whose education has been funded out of the public purse, emigrate as soon as they leave college, what benefit has the country reaped from the investment? Questions like this pose serious threats to the reform process. Unless brain drain is considered at the policy development stage, it may come to complicate decisions about investment in higher education and it could provoke strong political opposition.

To reiterate, the point here is that consideration of the politics of reform as well as its technical aspects is crucial. In this connection, Pakistan's efforts at higher education reform provide some instructive examples.

As in much of the rest of the developing world, Pakistan had traditionally taken education to mean predominantly primary and secondary schooling. Both quantity and quality of higher education delivery were woefully inadequate for the country's needs. Governance and management structures and practices, inefficient use of resources, inadequate funding, poor recruitment practices, a lack of attention to research, and the politicization of faculty, staff, and students all blocked the path to efficient delivery. Reform was urgently needed.

The complex political situation in Pakistan also complicates reform. The country is effectively ruled by a military dictatorship and a fairly chaotic bureaucracy that makes it difficult to achieve anything quickly – not a promising context for implementing a far-reaching reform process.

Recently, a group of reform-minded Pakistanis met to address this situation. They included representatives from academia, civil society, business and the Boston Group (an American-based Pakistani think tank). Going beyond the usual technical aspects of reform, they also addressed the political aspects of reform and its implementation. To be sure, they made recommendations on technical matters such as the length of Bachelor's degrees, how much new funding was required (and the creation of an endowment to help raise it), delinking faculty pay from the Government's pay scales, and peer review of faculty to ensure that excellence is rewarded (more details of the technical steps can be found on the Task Force for Higher Education website at www.tfhe.net). But they also dealt thoughtfully, systematically and respectfully with the opposition to change, which consisted of a formidable array of higher education institutions reluctant to adapt, politicians and government officials opposed to the involvement of the Boston Group, and many people opposed to President Musharraf's regime in general.

In order to effect change in such a system, the Pakistan Higher Education Task Force relied on what they describe as an entrepreneurial model. This model seeks to promote and encourage 'social entrepreneurs', who seek out 'strategic points of entry' into the reform process. Thus, instead of trying to get everybody lined up together at the outset and then undertake every part of the reform process at once, individuals and small groups take the initiative and, by effecting change in one small part of the system, attempt to trigger larger changes in other areas.

In this model, it is possible to initiate reform without government support, and even without the support of the whole higher education community. By creating and promoting early success stories, the pioneers can encourage others to become active and build the momentum that will eventually get the politicians' attention.

The Pakistan Task Force model appears to have made a favourable impression on the country's leaders. On hearing the report and recommendations of the Task Force, President Musharraf announced an immediate 1 billion rupee (currently about US$18 million) increase in the budget allocation for public universities in the current fiscal year, an increase of a third over the previous budget. He also approved the establishment of a Higher Education Commission and an overall doubling of government grants to higher education by 2004/2005. The Pakistan reform is still at an early stage, but the example is a promising one, because it shows what can be done even from unpromising beginnings. Higher education reform does not happen overnight, but globalization is changing the world so fast there is no time to waste in embarking on reform.

The course adopted by Pakistan is not necessarily the best or the only approach to reform, and it is not clear that it can be replicated elsewhere. But we do need to pay attention to the reform process and think as deeply about the politics as we do about the technical issues.

In sum, it is time to resolve the contradictions surrounding higher education in the developing world. We need those responsible for education as a whole, and those responsible for higher education in particular, to start working in the same direction. Only then can they propel their countries forward to help shape the path and process of globalization and take full advantage of globalization's potential.

NOTES

This chapter is based on a speech delivered at the University of Laval conference on Globalization: What Issues Are at Stake for Universities, September 18–21 2002, Quebec City, Canada. The author is grateful to Tariq Banuri, Gilles Breton, Michel Lambert, Mamphela Ramphele, Larry Rosenberg, Henry Rosovsky, and Mark Weston for helpful comments and discussions.

1. http://www.southcentre.org/publications/ecommerce/ecommerce-09.htm; http://www.oxfam.org.hk/english/campaigns/food_hunger/geneng_food.shtml

United Nations Millennium Development Goals and Targets

Goal 1: Eradicate extreme poverty and hunger
Target 1 Halve, between 1990 and 2015, the proportion of people whose income is less than one dollar a day.

Target 2 Halve, between 1990 and 2015, the proportion of people who suffer from hunger.

Goal 2: Achieve universal primary education
Target 3 Ensure that, by 2015, children everywhere, boys and girls alike, will be able to complete a full course of primary schooling.

Goal 3: Promote gender equality and empower women
Target 4 Eliminate gender disparity in primary and secondary education, preferably by 2005, and at all levels of education no later than 2015.

Goal 4: Reduce child mortality
Target 5 Reduce by two thirds, between 1990 and 2015, the under-five mortality rate.

Goal 5: Improve maternal health
Target 6 Reduce by three quarters, between 1990 and 2015, the maternal mortality ratio.

Goal 6: Combat HIV/AIDS, malaria and other diseases
Target 7 Have halted by 2015 and begun to reverse the spread of HIV/AIDS.

Target 8 Have halted by 2015 and begun to reverse the incidence of malaria and other major diseases.

Goal 7: Ensure environmental sustainability

Target 9   Integrate the principles of sustainable development into country policies and programmes and reverse the loss of environmental resources.

Target 10   Halve by 2015 the proportion of people without sustainable access to safe drinking water.

Target 11   By 2020 to have achieved a significant improvement in the lives of at least 100 million slum dwellers.

Goal 8: Develop a global partnership for development

Target 12   Develop further an open, rule-based, predictable, non-discriminatory trading and financial system.

Target 13   Address the special needs of the least developed countries.

Target 14   Address the special needs of landlocked countries and small island developing States (through the Programme of Action for the Sustainable Development of Small Island Developing States and the outcome of the twenty-second special session of the General Assembly).

Target 15   Deal comprehensively with the debt problems of developing countries through national and international measures in order to make debt sustainable in the long term.

Target 16   In cooperation with developing countries, develop and implement strategies for decent and productive work for youth.

Target 17   In cooperation with pharmaceutical companies, provide access to affordable essential drugs in developing countries.

Target 18   In cooperation with the private sector, make available the benefits of new technologies, especially information and communications.

10. Globalization and its Implications for Universities in Developing Countries

Goolam Mohamedbhai

Universities are international in their outlook by their very nature, and those in the developing world have always considered themselves as part of a global structure. Indeed, the majority of universities in former colonies have been patterned on those in the North; most of their faculty have at least one qualification from a university in the North; the institutions with which they have the largest number of collaborative ventures and exchange programmes are located in the North; and the curricula and programme structures of their degrees are not very different from those in Northern universities. So one might think that universities in the developing countries already follow global trends.

The above, however, are aspects of 'internationalization' of higher education, not 'globalization'. The latter is very different from the former. Globalization has resulted in higher education being regarded as a commercial product, governed essentially by market forces, and has brought in the concept of competitiveness. The results of commercialization and competitiveness – concepts that until recently were considered anathemas in the university world – can be the very opposite of those of internationalization. There is now the proposal by the World Trade Organization (WTO) to liberalize trade in education services (including higher education) through the General Agreement on Trade in Services (GATS). While no doubt globalization may have some positive effects from the point of view of increasing access in higher education and reducing the knowledge gap in developing countries, it equally has negative aspects that can seriously threaten universities in those countries.

ENROLMENT

Perhaps the greatest change that has occurred in universities in developing countries over the past decades has been the large increase in student enrolment. This is due to higher output from secondary schools, greater participation of women in higher education, a growing private sector demand for graduates and the exorbitant costs of acquiring education in foreign countries, especially those in the North. As a result, universities have been under enormous pressure to increase access and have had to double or even triple their intake. Even with such increases, developing countries, especially in Africa, have still not attained satisfactory participation rates in higher education. At a time when countries in the North are aiming to have about 50 per cent of their population in the age group 18–24 participating in higher education, most African countries have barely reached participation rates of 10 per cent. The pressure for greater access therefore continues, as it is recognized that the knowledge gap between the rich and poor countries can only be narrowed, and national development sustained, if the participation rate in higher education is of the order of 20 per cent.

PUBLIC FUNDING

However, the increased enrolment in universities in developing countries, most of which are publicly funded, has not been matched by a proportionate increase in public funding, and the universities now find themselves stretched almost to the limit. The reluctance of governments to fund higher education was at one time influenced by the stand taken by some funding/donor agencies (which was subsequently revised) that developing countries derive maximum economic benefits by channelling their funds into primary and secondary education sectors rather than the higher education sector, leaving the latter largely to fend for itself. With governments placing greater emphasis on privatization and the market economy, there has also been the increasing tendency to believe that higher education is a 'private good', that graduates benefit personally from higher education by improving their employability and social status, and that, as the main beneficiaries, they should finance their own studies, thus relieving the public sector of that burden. There is finally the hard reality that the economic situation in most developing countries is such that the state is unable to provide the additional funding required to further expand the public tertiary education sector.

At the same time universities in the North had started to function as corporate entities, putting into practice such principles as quality management and efficiency, and fiercely promoting revenue-generating activities. Private, for-profit universities started to emerge and higher education, now regarded as a commercial commodity, came to be recognized as a profitable business. This encouraged even new providers from outside the higher education sector to enter the market. Distance Learning started to gain prominence, and new information and communication technologies made it possible for courses to be delivered on-line via the Internet. Then came the WTO and GATS, promoting free and liberalized trade in higher education across national borders.

FOREIGN PROVIDERS

The ground in developing countries was therefore fertile and the conditions favourable for enterprising foreign providers of higher education from developed countries to move in. And they have, in some countries in a significant way. In addition to for-profit institutions, many foreign universities, also cash-strapped and pressed for increasing enrolment (especially of foreign students), have seized the opportunity to capture the market in developing countries. The developing countries have generally welcomed the foreign providers, in some cases even facilitated their entry, as a means of making higher education more accessible to their population without any increase in public funding.

This has given rise to what is now termed 'transnational education' or the provision of education to learners in a country different from the provider. There are broadly speaking two main methods of delivery of higher education by foreign providers to learners in developing countries. The first is delivery through their physical presence in the host country. This is done either by establishing a local branch or satellite campus or by using a local partner (a private college or institution but very rarely a local, public-funded university) for course delivery. In some cases, part of the course is delivered in the developing country and part of it in the country of the foreign provider.

The second method of delivery is through 'cross-border delivery', where the course is delivered by the provider remaining in the foreign country to the students in the developing country. International distance education and e-learning fall under this category. An increasing number of students in developing countries are opting for cross-border delivery of higher education, although in many instances the foreign provider (an open university or a virtual university) is also located in a developing country.

A noteworthy point is that foreign providers offer courses mostly in professional areas such as management, accountancy, finance, law and information technology, which do not require the establishment of large-scale infrastructure.

EFFECTS AND IMPLICATIONS

It must be acknowledged that foreign providers have helped in increasing access to higher education in developing countries, as governments in those countries are finding it difficult to provide additional resources to local universities to meet the increasing demand for higher education. The foreign providers have particularly helped in promoting lifelong learning and continuing professional development. Learners have also welcomed the availability locally of programmes of foreign universities at a significantly lower cost than if they were to travel to study abroad. This has been particularly beneficial to mature students, who are able to study part-time while working and staying with their families. Cross-border delivery through virtual education has revolutionized higher education in the sense that learners can now communicate directly with their tutors and other fellow-learners in real time. The fact that fewer students travel abroad to study also has a positive effect on the net foreign currency outflow.

But the globalization of higher education can also have negative effects on developing countries and their universities. First, globalization can undermine the very purpose for which universities in the Third World were created, namely to assist in the economic, social and cultural development of their respective countries. Foreign providers do not share the same national values and priorities. Their purpose is solely to provide education in the most cost-effective way. Universities are not places where one simply goes to be educated. They are institutions where the young meet to learn, reflect and debate on their society, and to develop intellectually, culturally and physically. Campus-based higher education provides the students with a unique personal experience that helps them to become better citizens later. Universities also undertake research relevant to local needs, and interact with and provide valuable services to their communities by making their resources available and through advice and consultancy. These functions cannot effectively be provided by foreign institutions through their corporate delivery approach. Indeed, virtual education even calls into question the need to have a physical campus, as learners benefit from all the necessary facilities (laboratories, tutorials, discussion groups) virtually.

Second, globalization raises the important issue of national control and planning of higher education. While universities in developing countries need to have autonomy in their academic activities and their faculty must enjoy academic freedom, nevertheless, since they are public-funded institutions, they need to be accountable to their governments and must respond to overall national education plans. There is a real danger that once higher education has been liberalized, it is the rules of GATS and WTO that will regulate the market. Developing countries will be flooded with foreign and private providers delivering essentially profitable subjects. In those areas, they will pose as serious competitors to local universities, leaving the latter to deal with non-profitable subjects in arts, humanities, science and technology that are so vital for a country's development. This could lead to the abandonment of some subjects in local universities for which the market demand is poor. The effect will be especially dramatic for small developing countries having a single or only a few universities. A 'McDonaldization' of higher education will then ensue.

Third, many of the foreign providers offer courses of dubious quality and function as 'diploma mills'. Since they are commercially motivated they can often exploit and mislead local students. In some cases, even courses delivered by well-known universities of the North have been found to be of substandard quality. In the case of delivery by distance education, very often there is a lack of adequate learner support locally, with the students left to fend for themselves as best they can. Few developing countries have effective mechanisms in place to control the quality of courses delivered by foreign providers in the context of liberalized higher education.

Fourth, foreign providers will draw most of their faculty from the host country. They will be in a position to offer enticing salaries and may attract the best-qualified (but poorly paid) faculty members away from local universities. As it is, most universities in developing countries are already facing a serious problem of recruiting or even retaining good faculty, and the situation will worsen with the arrival of foreign providers, thus affecting the quality of delivery of their courses. Foreign providers could also outsource faculty from local universities on a part-time basis. Those staff members, overburdened with teaching, will then not be in a position to undertake research and development activities in their expert areas, to the detriment of their professional development, their universities and their countries.

Finally, the presence of a large number of foreign providers could further increase the social divide in developing countries. Affluent students and those from the middle class will opt for enrolment in private, foreign institutions, leaving the public institutions, which are already poorly funded and which cannot afford to offer the best academic environment, to cater for the poorer students. Local employers, especially those in the private sector, may prefer to employ graduates with foreign qualifications, so that the best jobs will go to the latter, again widening the social gap.

ACTIONS

The question that arises is whether globalization and the wave of liberalization of higher education can be contained and, if not, what steps countries and universities in developing countries should take to minimize its negative effects. It must be accepted that transnational education is now a reality. In any case, as mentioned earlier, it is unlikely that developing countries will be in a position to significantly increase access to higher education and achieve the desired participation rate without the contribution of private and foreign providers. And globalization can have beneficial effects. What is important is to ensure that the contribution of those providers is sufficiently controlled so that it does not hamper the development objectives of the country.

The potential dangers of complete liberalization of higher education, and especially of the negative impact of such action on higher education systems in developing countries, are now becoming known worldwide. It is comforting to note that a significant number of leading academics in the developed world have openly voiced their objections to the inclusion of education services under GATS. Similar reservations were expressed by the Association of Universities and Colleges of Canada, the American Council on Education, the European University Association and the Council for Higher Education Accreditation (which together represent over 3,500 higher education institutions in North America and Europe) in a joint declaration made in September 2001. In that declaration, they advised their respective governments not to make any commitments in higher education services in the context of GATS. Academics and university associations in the Third World must join hands with them and, in turn, voice their concern to their governments and at relevant international forums. A few developing countries have already made their schedule of commitments in higher education services under the GATS. Those that have not yet done so should have thorough consultation with their national universities before listing their commitments so that they are fully aware of the consequences.

It is essential for governments of developing countries to acknowledge that there is a 'public good' aspect to universities, that universities play a central role in the development of a nation, that they benefit the society at large in addition to individual recipients and that they therefore need to be supported to fulfil their mission. It is accepted by all stakeholders that universities must operate more efficiently, must be managed more professionally, must try to supplement their public grants with self-generated funds, must be accountable and must respond to the needs of the world of work. But governments must realize that national universities will never be in a position to be completely independent of public funds, that they need to be provided with adequate resources to recruit and retain good faculty, and to have satisfactory academic facilities for teaching and research. Only a strong and well-performing local university, appreciated locally and recognized internationally, will be in a position to compete with and stand up to foreign, private providers.

In order to control the operation of foreign providers and protect students from bogus institutions, there must be a national regulatory framework. Very few developing countries, especially those in Africa, have such a framework in place. At best they might have a quality assurance and/or an accreditation system in operation but these generally cover only the national higher education sector. Setting up a regulatory framework is a complex task, although Hong Kong (China) and Malaysia for example, have succeeded in laying down regulations for transnational education. What is perhaps required is a regional or even international approach to the problem. The Association of African Universities, for example, could help in formulating guidelines for a regulatory system, after examining existing systems that have been operating successfully in different countries. The regulation of cross-border delivery of higher education, especially virtual education, is even more complex, and requires special attention.

So far most of the foreign providers have avoided collaboration with existing local universities. This could be partly due to the understandable reluctance of a local university to be associated with the delivery of a course of another, foreign university. And yet, such collaboration could be beneficial to both institutions and the country. They could pool their resources and run courses leading to joint awards by the two institutions. Funding and donor agencies in developed countries should promote such collaborative ventures between universities in the North and South.

Many developing countries, especially small ones, do not have the capacity to develop distance education, especially virtual education, and local learners are increasingly dependent on courses delivered from developed countries. Regional and even international cooperation among developing countries can help in capacity-building in those areas. There is, for example, the interesting proposal to create a virtual university for small states of the Commonwealth, whereby existing local universities will collaborate, through a consortium, to build up their own infrastructural and delivery capacity in virtual education. Funding and donor agencies should encourage and support such collaborative initiatives.

Finally there is an urgent need for research and country studies to be carried out to determine the effect of globalization on higher education in developing countries. Some of the issues to be examined are: What proportion of tertiary sector students take courses delivered by foreign providers? What are the views of students on the quality of courses of these providers? What are the local resources used by foreign providers? Is there any quality control mechanism for foreign providers? What have been the effects felt by local universities? What are the views of local employers on graduates of foreign providers as compared to those of local universities?

CONCLUSION

Sustained global development can only take place when there is sustained development in all individual countries, as globalization has created a situation where all countries of the world are interdependent. Universities have an important role to play in promoting sustainable national development. However, globalization has created some serious challenges for universities in developing countries.

Some forty to fifty years ago, universities in developed countries assisted the former colonies that had just become independent in establishing universities that would help them in their development. Would it not be more appropriate for universities in the North once again to collaborate with and assist their sister-institutions in the South to overcome some of the challenges of globalization, rather than compete with them?

BIBLIOGRAPHY

Altbach, P. G. 2001. *Higher Education and the WTO: Globalization Run Amok.* Newsletter No. 23, Center for International Higher Education, Boston College, Spring.

Anon. 2002. *WTO: Trade in Services.* Working group on educational services: Position paper for Mauritius, May. Mauritius, Tertiary Education Commission. 20 pp.

Aponte, E. 1998. Globalization, Integration, Economic Policy and Higher Education in North America and the Carribean: Nafta's Impact in the Periphery. *Educacion Global,* Vol. 2, pp. 133–49.

AUCC, ACE, EUA & CHEA. 2001. Joint declaration on higher education and the General Agreement on Trade in Services, 28 September. *IAU Newsletter,* Vol. 8, No. 1, pp. 6–7.

Commonwealth of Learning. 2002. *A Virtual University for Small States of the Commonwealth: Report of the 'Technical Advisery Committee'.* July, in draft. 37 pp.

Lenn, M. P. 1998. The New Technologies and Borderless Higher-education: The Quality Imperative. *Higher Education in Europe,* Vol. 23, No. 2, pp. 241–51.

McBurnie, G. and Ziguras, C. 2001., The Regulation of Transnational Higher Education in Southeast Asia: Case Studies of Hong Kong, Malaysia and Australia. *Higher Education,* No. 42, pp. 85–105.

Neave, G. 2001. *Globalization, Higher Education and the IAU.* Paper presented at the 64th IAU Administrative Board Meeting, Mexico, 13–15 November. 23 pp.

Powar, K. B. *WTO, GATS and higher education: an Indian Perspective.* Association of Indian Universities Occasional Paper 2002/1. 21 pp.

Sawyerr, A. 2002. The Public Good in African Higher Education: Select Issues for Policy. Keynote speech at 'Higher Education at the Crossroads: a Policy Consultation on Higher Education in Africa', Dakar, Senegal, February. 10 pp.

Scott, P. 1999. Globalization and the University. *CRE-action,* No. 115, pp. 35–46.

Skilbeck, M. 1997. Higher Education in a Changing Environment: Regional, National and Trans-national Issues. *Tertiary Education and Management,* Vol. 3, No. 2, pp. 101–11.

Van Damme, D. 2001. Higher Education in the Age of Globalization. Paper presented at 'Expert Meeting on the Impact of Globalization on Quality Assurance, Accreditation and the Recognition of Qualifications in Higher Education'. UNESCO, Paris, 10–11 September. 12 pp.

11. Globalization Apartheid: The Role of Higher Education in Development

Teboho Moja

Globalization as a concept is used in this paper not from an ideological point of view but rather as an economic process that tries to integrate world economies. Globalization – particularly the removal of barriers to free trade, and the integration of national economies – has potential as a force for reducing poverty levels in the world. The problems in reaching those goals (poverty reduction) are mainly due to policies adopted, the management of those processes, the politics in decision making and lack of representation from those whose lives are directly affected by globalization (Stiglitz, 2002; Castells, 1996). Views from the South that could inform those policies are often ignored by international development agencies. Academic debates on these issues try to incorporate other views, but the outcomes of such debates seldom have direct impact on development policies.

At the World Summit on Sustainable Development (WSSD), President Mbeki, addressing a crowd of protesters, mentioned that the greatest enemy to development is global apartheid.[1] Representatives at the WSSD objected to this use of the concept of apartheid because of its association with South Africa's former government's deliberate discrimination against people from different racial backgrounds. The implications are that there is no deliberate intention to treat countries differently in the new economic process. The issue is debatable because there is evidence of global apartheid: the gap between the rich and the poor has widened in the past decades as poverty levels have risen.

There is evidence of the devastating effects of globalization on developing countries as the poverty gap has increased despite the fact that globalization was meant to benefit all members of the global community. To date it is estimated that about 40 per cent of families in the world survive on less than one dollar per day. This is in contrast to the subsidies given to farmers in countries like the United States, where the subsidy is about a dollar per day per animal. The G8 Summit of June 2002 refused to address the issue of subsidies provided for in the United States Farm Bill, which perpetuates the overproduction and export dumping that undermine agriculture in Africa. The new Farm Bill announced around April 2002 aims to increase US farm subsidies by $35 billion, which translates to more than $20,000 for each farmer (*Mail and Guardian*, May 2002). The negative impact of globalization has been felt more by those in developing countries. For example, Africa has had a 4 per cent decline in GDP, a decline in per capita income that has resulted in a drop of living standards. This has happened within a context where world income has increased annually by 2.5 per cent (Stiglitz, 2002, p. 5).

Apartheid was defined as an empowering strategy through the separation of races, the unequal distribution of resources and privileges, and the preservation of cultures. Policies were decided upon by the dominant minority that held power, which tried to justify the need for people of different races to develop separately, while remaining connected and being dependent on each other. The global economy operates with comparable strategies and policies to those that were adopted by the repressive former government of South Africa. The change to power sharing in South Africa was brought about through strategies that included the mobilization of mass protests. International activists have adopted similar strategies, as shown in scenes of conflict at World Trade Organization meetings (Seattle, 1999; Genoa, 2001), United Nations Conferences (Durban, 2001; Johannesburg, 2002), World Bank and IMF meetings in Washington, D.C. (2001, 2002).

World politics are intertwined with policies for development and impact negatively on development strategies. Speakers at the WSSD complained about how the Summit agenda was dominated by EU and US views that imposed their own perceptions and definition of humanity (South African Broadcasting Corporation news, 31 August 2002). At the end of the Summit, the United States stood alone due to its hard line, refusing to set targets for the eradication of poverty and undoing environmental damage as part of the strategy for sustainable development (*Sunday Times*, 1 September 2002).

Globalization is characterized by increased connectedness as well as major inequities between countries and within countries. The digital divide between the North and South that is often presented in globalization debates is real, but it is also problematic in the sense that the division cannot only be explained in terms of the division between the North and South, because there are cities in the North that are worse or similar to some cities in the South. There is poverty and illiteracy in the North and instances where people live under worse conditions than those in the South. There are also pockets of technological development in both the North and the South that alter the parameters to the 'haves' and 'have nots' rather than just the North and the South.

Overall, globalization apartheid has had a devastating effect on developing countries. There have been acknowledgements from the World Bank and the British Department for International Development that the benefits of globalization are not being passed on to sub-Saharan Africa and instead globalization has exacerbated many of Africa's problems (*Mail and Guardian*, 31 May 2002). Trade relations are reported to be unfavourable for Africa, and as a result the percentage of trade has dropped in the last two decades. There are warnings of the possibility that developing countries are at risk of being excluded from the dynamics of the world economy (World Bank Report, 2002; Castells, 1996). Stiglitz (2002) argues that to reverse the situation there is a need to radically rethink policies imposed on developing countries in areas such as trade agreements. He further argues that for globalization to benefit all, there is a need to share growth in a more equitable way.

HIGHER EDUCATION AND DEVELOPMENT

The role of education in development is becoming unclear, with rhetoric dominating debates on globalization and development. So far, the lack of economic development mainly in countries of the South has been blamed, *inter alia*, on low participation rates in higher education. In response some East Asian countries have adopted a strategy of designing their education systems to help close the knowledge and technology gap between them and the North. Their economies improved until the recent financial crisis that impacted negatively on those countries.

There is a need to raise the issue of the role of higher education in development in the context of regions such as Africa, where nearly half of sub-Saharan Africa's 600 million people live on less than one dollar a day, more than a third of children are malnourished, people are dying of AIDS and there have been minimal improvements in education and health. There is data that correlate levels of development to levels of participation in education. There are convincing arguments for increasing participation rates in education as both a human right and a strategy for development. These arguments have been presented in different forums discussing strategies for development and remain unconnected to debates by intellectuals in the education field.

The role of higher education in the development agendas, such as those of the United Nations Millennium Development Goals or the WSSD, is unclear and this is a matter of concern. The United Nations report on sustainable development warned that education was in danger of being forgotten. The 1992 Rio meeting on sustainable development had put education on the agenda but failed to specify the role of higher education. At the 2002 Johannesburg meeting, higher education stakeholders participated through a consortium referred to as 'The Linked Consortia for Environmental and Development – Industry and Urban Areas' (Luced-I&UA) as a way of ensuring that higher education becomes part of the development agenda.[2] An interesting observation is that, apart from Denmark, countries from the North were not represented on the consortium.[3]

Another example of lack of clarity about the role of higher education in development is the notable absence of higher education participation in the development of Africa's renewal strategy 'The New Partnership for Africa's Development' (NEPAD). The presentation of this strategy to leaders of powerful nations in Canada recently by a delegation of three African heads of state led by Thabo Mbeki did not receive the anticipated response of a high commitment to supporting the development strategy for Africa.[4] Five heads of state presented the plan to the United Nations General Assembly in 2002.[5] There was criticism of the plan, particularly its failure to consult widely within the continent, but it received widespread support. NEPAD represents a shift in strategy by African governments from relying on aid for development to demanding a change in trading relationships between the North and South, because trade has more potential for development than aid. Planned NEPAD projects require huge amounts of money to implement and partnership with the North is sought in that regard.

In the globalizing economy, higher education has featured on the WTO agenda not for its contribution to development but more as a service to trade, or as a commodity that can boost income for countries with the ability to trade in this area and export their higher education programmes. Higher education has become a multi-billion dollar market as the quantity of education is increasing rapidly and is reported to be doubling every five years. It has been noted that the export of higher education services has contributed significantly to the economy of the United States. In 1999 it is estimated that the United States, as the largest provider of education services, earned $8.5 billion of the $30 billion market, from this trade alone (Hayward, 2002). The share for Asia is estimated at $10 billion.

Higher education has in the past contributed to development by providing national economies with necessary human resources, but it has been criticized for not dealing directly with poverty reduction issues. The recent World Bank report on higher education, still in draft form, presents an argument for the indirect role that higher education can play in development and in poverty reduction as part of the Bank's development strategy. Three key arguments are presented in the report. The first is that higher education can contribute to economic growth by supplying the necessary human resources for a knowledge-driven economy, by generating knowledge, and by promoting access to and use of knowledge. The second argument is that higher education has the potential to increase access to education and in turn increase the employability of those who have the skills for a knowledge-driven economy. The third argument is that higher education can play a role in supporting basic and secondary education by supplying those subsectors with trained personnel and contributing to the development of the curriculum (World Bank report, 2002, p. xi).

There is a need to rethink the role of higher education in national development as national economies are slowly being replaced by a global economy and national higher education is being slowly replaced by global systems of higher education. Higher education's role has shifted to supporting an economy that is knowledge intensive at a global level. The relevance of higher education systems at local level needs to be rethought in the framework of their relevance in the global context, hence the question as to whether they are still relevant to development at a local level. The issue is of concern as the public good of systems of higher education operating at a global level is debatable. There has been a renewal of higher education systems in the countries of the South and a renewed interest by the donor agencies operating in Africa in supporting higher education. At national levels new reform policies are being developed, and at institutional levels new leadership has embarked on processes to revive their institutions and write new strategic development plans. International agencies such as the World Bank have also revised their policies towards supporting higher education and have come to accept the view that there is need for investment at all levels of education as a strategy for promoting development. The changes taking place have put considerable emphasis on the need for accountability to society beyond financial accountability, demand for intellectual leadership and on partnership that could contribute to development.

PROMOTING COOPERATION WITHIN A COMPETITIVE ENVIRONMENT

The more we become integrated in the world economy, the more we are under pressure to increase our competitiveness and the more we need to have education of higher quality than we have today (Enrique Iglesias, President of the Inter-American Development Bank, in a speech delivered at the Latin America Basic Education Summit (LABES), 7 March 2001).

One of the key features of globalization is increased competition, which has become a driving force for innovation and entrepreneurship. Competition in higher education has increased and has become unfair. Countries of the North with their competitive advantages compete with countries of the South for the best students, faculty, administrators and researchers. Intellectual resources from the South are being drained in the process. The main sources of high-level skilled labour for the thriving global economy have been the developing countries, and the Russian Federation during its transition to a capitalist economy (*The Chronicle*, September 8 2000). Articles in *The Chronicle of Higher Education* have reported on concerns over the brain drain from developing countries. In one of them, Burton Bollag estimates that Africa has lost 100,000 people with specialized skills to the West, including about 23,000 qualified academic professionals each year. The countries reported to have lost the most academics are Egypt, Ghana, Kenya, Nigeria and South Africa. The Russian Federation reports a loss of 30,000 researchers (*The Chronicle*, 8 September 2000). Brain drain is reported to be among the greatest obstacles to development (Buckley, 2002; Wachira, 2001).

Countries from the South are at risk of being further marginalized if their higher education institutions fail to participate in the knowledge production networks and activities that would make them relevant and more responsive to the needs of a new economy. Concern has been raised by academics from the South about lack of collegiality among academics within a competitive environment. Competition has resulted in student losses to private for-profit higher education, loss of jobs and, in some cases, the threat of closure of institutions. Competition in academia has continued to perpetuate the negative effects of globalization, such as increasing inequality both between academics within institutions and between academics in different institutions and countries (Moja and Cloete, 2001).

The regulation of goods and services in a globalizing context and in general has also become a problem for many countries and it costs countries heavily, despite the adoption of tough laws by organizations such as the World Trade Organization. International companies and institutions are flooding developing countries with cheap products. In higher education trade, inferior programmes are offered at high prices to students in the South, especially in countries where there are no quality control mechanisms in place. Even in situations where there are some control measures, there are institutions that manage to slip through and students are short-changed. The situation has become serious, and some countries find it difficult to protect what they value in education in the same way that countries in the North do. South Africa has responded by declaring a moratorium on new partnerships in distance education during a period of transformation while putting quality control mechanisms in place.[6]

To promote cooperation within a competitive environment it is necessary to consider current institutional responses to global changes and the perceived threat posed by increased competition. Universities in the South have responded in different ways to the challenges they face from globalization. Moja and Cloete (2001) categorized the responses based on their study of the higher education landscape in South Africa as follows:

The need to compete and increase market share

This guides developments in institutions that have reluctantly embraced the changes and have responded by adopting market strategies for change. Attention is paid to strategic planning and to recognizing and distinguishing between the core business and non-core business, resulting in the outsourcing of non-core business activities. Students are treated as clients, budgeting is organized into cost centres and management emphasizes efficiency in all operations at an institution. New funding mechanisms are sought, including a push for contract research in knowledge production.

The need to focus on local changes and ignore global changes

This is recognized in institutions that have been focusing more on internal politics driven by recent political changes in South Africa. These institutions have been restructuring their governance structures to bring them into line with legislative requirements. Due to conflicts between stake-holders and leadership, to transformation demands on leadership, and to financial problems, such institutions have as yet not even started responding to the global changes taking place.

The need to fight new cultural imperialists

This has priority in institutions where there is a perceived threat of a takeover by foreign providers of higher education. Some institutions have asked the government to protect them from 'foreign invaders' and the government has responded by imposing a moratorium on new distance education programmes, as already mentioned. Other institutions have opted to fight by competing in the global world; one South African institution, for example, was granted a contract (against competition from British institutions) to offer distance health education programmes in Turkey and Israel. Other strategies for fighting have been to form partnerships with the private sector in delivering educational programmes to masses of students, tapping new sources and increasing institutional budgets.

National responses to globalization vary from innovations driven by the need for survival to increased competition and becoming more entrepreneurial. Institutions in Europe particularly have opted to become more entrepreneurial and the newly appointed president of New York University has been pushing an agenda for an enterprise university.[7] The newly formed European Consortia of Innovative Universities (ECIU) is another example, as is the emerging literature on entrepreneur univer-sities. There are countries that have embraced the changes, and some developing countries have even signed up to participate in the General Agreement on Trade in Services (GATS). Hong Kong (China) for example has opted to embrace the changes taking place and capitalize on the oppor-tunities offered to increase access to higher education. Countries that have been unable to increase participation rates due to financial constraints have also opted for opening up their countries to global foreign providers as a cheaper option than investing in the needed infrastructure.

The issue to be raised is whether it is possible to cooperate within a competitive environment. The private sector offers some lessons on strategic partnerships when these are necessary in order to become more compet-itive. In higher education, opportunities for cooperation are created by the emergence of multiple, networked, global knowledge-production sites as higher education increasingly loses the monopoly of knowledge production. Two challenges arise for universities in the South. The first is to become part of the networks, and the second is to produce or use knowledge for development purposes. With the latter, institutions are finding themselves paying more attention to meeting the need for increased access at the expense of research. Faculty teaching loads have been increasing, leaving little room for research, as survival has become more dependent on fee-paying students.

Universities from the North have generally responded to globalization by establishing partnerships with other knowledge producers and by participation in innovation hubs. Universities in the South need to be part of the new arrangements being forged in the North in knowledge production, dissemination and reconfiguration. Emerging social relations so far largely exclude universities from the South. There is a need to include universities of the South in the new transinstitutional arrangements for the development of knowledge-production sites and multiple agencies involved in the production and dissemination of knowledge (Moja and Cloete, 2001, p. 246). If there is no cooperation in involving universities from the South in such arrangements, there is a danger that the gap between the poor and the rich nations will continue to widen.

Universities from the South have already been indirectly affected by new market operations in new information production and dissemination. Universities from the North have recruited the best students, faculty and researchers from their counterparts in the South. Some institutions, in South Africa for example, have also lost their best senior administrators to countries in the North and their best students to the institutions that had the best facilities provided by the former discriminatory government. There is a need to cooperate in capacity building for those institutions that in some cases have paid little or no attention to knowledge production due to financial constraints. Partnership between universities could contribute to capacity building in knowledge production and use of knowledge, in delivering and disseminating knowledge to masses of students, and in contributing to the development of human resources with high-level skills, which in turn could contribute to development.

In considering cooperative and partnership arrangements, universities in the North need to address some of the concerns raised by universities in the South and their responses to global changes and increased competition. First, there is general concern that with the changes taking place globally, countries of the South are at risk of having their local concerns overlooked or ignored. The response in some instances has been to shift from basic research to applied research. For example, knowledge production trends in South Africa indicate a shift to addressing more national concerns. There is evidence that overall knowledge production figures have dropped, but institutions are conducting more contract research directed at strategic (socio-economic and industry) goals (Moja and Cloete, 2001, p. 255).

Second, there is concern over lack of sensitivity to the cultural bias of exported education and the negative impact competition could have on institutions as it erodes the best human resources, resulting in the decay or closure of institutions.

Third, there is concern over partnerships that might perpetuate inequalities among institutions and among students within the same institution. For example, private–public sector partnerships aimed at delivering education to the mass of the population could result in the short-changing of poor students who receive their education through those arrangements (Moja and Cloete, p. 251). The often-cited success story of innovations at Makerere University has been criticized in some quarters for creating inequalities among students taking the same courses. The partnership between Tufts University and Makerere University in delivering a political science course using technology allows some, but not all, students in the class to participate in interactions. The emerging inequalities have become common in countries with free higher education systems but with provision for the intake of fee-paying students to supplement institutional income.

Universities in the South need to take the initiative in strengthening themselves to be able to respond to the needs of a new global economy. An example of a model geared toward enabling universities to take the initiative in their revival is presented by the 'Foundation Partnership for Strengthening African Universities'. The partnership has decided to provide support to institutions in Africa that are responding to the new challenges posed by globalization and the need to respond to changing societal needs. The support is provided in the form of grants to institutions to develop and implement strategic plans, support for research on change in African universities, support to university leadership to participate in global networks and professional associations, and support for promoting debates on change and the role of universities in development.[8] The foundations provide support over an extended period whilst institutions work on mechanisms for sustainability.

Private and public sector cooperation could contribute to development. Higher education systems in some developing countries have remained largely elite despite recognition of the importance of increasing participation rates. The increasing demand for higher education has not been met, mainly due to budgetary constraints. The private sector has a role to play in providing higher education programmes to the majority of people who in the past could not access higher education. There could be private–public sector cooperation in this area, for example, the use of franchised material from the private sector by the public sector, or institutions contracting private-sector companies to deliver instruction in their areas of specialty. One success story is that of the partnership arrangement between a private company and a university in South Africa for first-year literacy classes for all students.

There is a need to encourage and support South-South linkages similar to those promoted through Luced-I&UA, in order to involve higher education institutions directly in development issues. The consortium aims to develop human resources through student, faculty and researcher exchanges, as well as through curriculum development, improved teaching methods, research networking, and joint projects in teaching and research.

CONCLUSION

It is desirable, given the disparities among nations and the need to ensure development, that development opportunities should be enabled by the 'haves' but owned by the 'have-nots'. Africa's new initiative for reconstruction, NEPAD, is based on the premise that Africans need to take the initiative in their own development. Historically, economic and political relations between the North and South have been underpinned by a pretence of helping developing countries improve their economic situation, but resulting in those countries getting poorer. Part of the solution is to let those who need help take ownership of development strategies, revise policies, change economic relationships between the rich and the poor, and encourage investment in poor countries.

There is a need for genuine commitment to development and mutually beneficial partnership arrangements between institutions in the North and those in the South. There is a need at a global level for the development of policies that will enable institutions to access technology and information. If such policies were put in place, then universities could participate and play their role in development.

It is necessary to rethink the role of higher education in development because it has become part of the enrichment agenda through agencies such as the WTO and GATS rather than part of the development agenda for sustainable development. For globalization to benefit all, there is a need to share growth in a more equitable way (Stiglitz, 2002).

NOTES

1. The summit was held in August-September 2002 in Johannesburg, South Africa.
2. The Linked Consortia for Environment and Development – Industry and Urban Areas (Luced-I&UA) is made up of four Consortia with nineteen universities as members from South Africa, Botswana, Denmark, Malaysia and Thailand. The Southern African Consortium of Universities for Development and Environment – Industry and Urban Areas (Sacode-I&UA) consists of the universities of Botswana, the Witwatersrand, Durban–Westville, Natal, Western Cape and Cape Town (*Mail and Guardian*, 30 August 2002).
3. The consortia was funded by the Danish Aid Agency DANIDA.
4. The June 2002 G8 Summit in Kananaskis, Canada, where $6 billion was offered towards the $64 billion needed for NEPAD projects. African leaders felt snubbed and the money offered was regarded as not new since it had previously been offered in Monterey, according to Steven Lewis, the UN special envoy. Phil Twyford, Director of Oxfam International, referred to it as re-packaged peanuts. The amount is equal to the South African military budget (*Mail and Guardian*, 12 July 2002).
5. Debated on 16 September 2002.
6. 'The National Plan lifts the moratorium on the introduction of new distance education programmes in contact institutions, which was imposed by the Minister in February 2000. However, from 2002, new student places in existing and new distance education programmes, including programmes offered as part of public–private partnerships, will only be funded if the programmes have been approved as part of the institution's plans. Institutions will also have to seek approval for the introduction of distance education programmes for which state subsidies are not required' (National Plan for Higher Education, February 2001).
7. For further reading I recommend Clark, Burton R. (1998): *Creating Entrepreneurial Universities: Organizational Pathways of Transformation*. Pergamon.
8. More information can be obtained from the participating foundations: Ford Foundation, Carnegie Corporation, Rockefeller Foundation and McArthur Foundation.

BIBLIOGRAPHY

Buckley, C. 2002. A report prepared to help plan the World Summit on Sustainable Development, to be held in Johannesburg in September 2002.

Castells, M. 1996. *The Information Age: Economy, Society and Culture.* Volume 1: *The Rise of the Network Society.* Oxford, Blackwell.

Clark, B. R. 1998. *Creating Entrepreneurial Universities: Organizational Pathways of Transformation.* New York, Pergamon.

Hayward, F. 2002. *An overview of Higher Education and GATS.* Draft Document for the American Council on Education in July.

Moja, T. and Cloete, N. 2001. Vanishing Borders and New Boundaries. In: Muller, J. Cloete, N. and Badat, S. (eds) 2001: *Challenges of Globalization: South African Debates with Manuel Castells.* Cape Town, Maskew Miller Longman.

Stiglitz, J. E. 2002. *Globalization and its Discontents.* New York, W. W. Norton.

Wachira, K. 2001. Academics' Emigration Said to Hurt Africa. *The Chronicle of Higher Education,* 2 November.

World Bank Report. 2002. *Constructing Knowledge Societies: New Challenges for Tertiary Education.* Washington D.C., World Bank.

PART FIVE

Globalization and Universities: New Players

12. Australian Universities as Enterprise Universities: Transformed Players on a Global Stage

Jan Currie

The word globalization elicits different reactions. It creates heroes of the likes of Jose Bové who bulldozed a half-built McDonald's restaurant in his hometown in southern France. In response to the unjust consequences of globalization, thousands of protestors take to the streets in anti-globalization marches. They struggle against transnational organizations such as the World Bank, the International Monetary Fund (IMF) and the World Trade Organization (WTO), and against members of groups such as the World Economic Forum and the G8, seen as winners in the globalization stakes. Even though the work of these globalizers is often veiled in secrecy, their message is clear: globalization in the form of free trade and economic liberalization is the key to eliminating poverty and creating wealth.

In this chapter, globalization is discussed in its economic form as a neo-liberal ideology. It encourages free trade and competition, the deregulation and privatization of the economy, along with a weakening of the public sector and trade unions. Moreover, it favours giving more power to businesses by making national borders permeable to the free flow of capital, goods and services (but not yet people). Globalization is commonly understood in terms of a global capitalist economy with cultural, political and economic dimensions. All these dimensions are structured by a rationality that is principally Western and economic. The exhortations from the globalizers are that countries must integrate into the global economy or sink into ever-deepening poverty.

In contrast, some Western economists suggest that globalization is doomed. For example, Professor John Gray of the London School of Economics, declares that the era of globalization is over:

The entire view of the world that supported the market's faith in globalization has melted down... Led by the United States, the world's richest states have acted on the assumption that people everywhere want to live as they do. As a result, they failed to recognize the deadly mixture of emotions – cultural resentment, the sense of injustice and a genuine rejection of western modernity – that lies behind the attacks on New York and Washington... The ideal of a universal civilisation is a recipe for unending conflict, and it is time it was given up (*The Economist*, 29 September 2001, p. 13).

In short, contradictory messages abound regarding globalization. A number of writers are beginning to see patterns of difference emerging in the responses of countries to global forces. Hall and Soskice (2001) demonstrate that market economies differ and their reactions to globalization have not produced the same policies. They identify at least three different patterns but write at length about two types: liberal market economies and coordinated market economies. They conclude that firms in these two market economies react differently to similar challenges.

There is a flow-on effect of globalizing policies for universities in these different types of economies. Due to lower public-sector funding in liberal market economies, universities are increasingly becoming more managerial and more entrepreneurial. However, most universities in European coordinated market economies have not followed the Anglo-American path of becoming entrepreneurial. Also, they have maintained a certain degree of democratic collegiality (Currie et al., 2002). A country's response to globalization appears to depend on the type of its market economy, the strength of its economy and the willingness of its citizenry to pay enough taxes to fund public institutions.

This chapter argues that globalization is not inexorable and it may not be necessary for universities to follow the path leading to greater managerialism. There are many risks involved for both countries and universities in adopting certain global practices. The chapter questions whether universities risk losing important values that served them well for centuries when they develop a corporate ethos that sits uneasily with scholarly, professional values.

During the past decade, competition for funding and privatization have transformed Australian universities, leading them to commercialize, to become more utilitarian, and to market their courses more aggressively in Australia and overseas. The chapter discusses three Australian universities, established in different eras, all restructuring to become more enterprising: Melbourne University (1855), a traditional university, recently developing Melbourne Private, and creating an alliance, Universitas 21, with Australian and overseas universities to deliver on-line courses; Monash University, established in 1961, becoming a multiversity by merging six campuses in Australia and building campuses in Malaysia and South Africa, and by capitalizing on satellite television and other new technologies extending open learning to students in Australia and overseas; and Murdoch University, a small university established in 1975, beginning as an alternative university and now struggling to be a global player in this competitive environment.

MELBOURNE, MONASH AND MURDOCH

Using Sklair's (2001) analysis of transnational corporations' turning themselves into global companies, I illustrate how three Australian universities developed into global institutions. Sklair measures globalization in terms of four criteria: foreign direct investment (FDI), world best practice (WBP), corporate citizenship and global vision. He asserts that the transnational capitalist class (TNC) is not made up only of executives of transnational corporations; it also includes globalizing professionals, such as vice-chancellors. Here, I weave a narrative of how the vice-chancellors of Melbourne, Monash and Murdoch strove to become global players and position their universities in the competitive market of higher education during the period 1996–2001. During this time, these vice-chancellors restructured their universities in terms of the norms and practices of global corporations, using the language of business to describe their visions.

Many Australian vice-chancellors model themselves on CEOs. They come close to Surowiecki's description of the new American CEOs as 'the Green Berets of corporate management', the 'swaggering outsider who rides into town to clean up the mess' that a previous CEO left behind. They exude a 'CEO hubris' that allows them to take charge and make decisions that Surowiecki suggests are not necessarily in the company's best interest (2001). McCarthy, in *Bullying: From Backyard to Boardroom*, portrays the Australian workplace as a culture where bullying is tolerated. He says 'the pressures of economic restructuring have collided with a vast number of poorly trained managers and some organizations under stress explicitly adopt bullying as a tactic to deal with their problems' (cited in Bachelard, 2001). Some academics suggest that this is happening in their universities.

All of the vice-chancellors, Alan Gilbert of Melbourne, David Robinson of Monash and Steven Schwartz of Murdoch, could be described as visionaries, looking to the long-term interests of their universities. Gilbert is described as a radical, preferring universities to become more self-reliant in a deregulated environment (Light, 2002). Schwartz exuded a similar rhetoric, ardently espousing a capitalist ideology and branding academics as socialists, left over from the 1960s.[1] The Centre for Independent Studies, a right-wing think tank, invited Gilbert and Schwartz to address the Centre about their visions of Australian universities. Robinson continued the work of predecessors, developing Monash into a global university, the largest in Australia with an enrolment of 47,000 students on eight campuses. Of these, 25.6 per cent were international students in 2001, and students at Monash speak over ninety languages. His vision was to have a Monash campus on every continent. He resigned before reaching that goal.

Both Gilbert and Schwartz encountered protests from students and staff. At Melbourne, the vice-chancellor's office was the site of student protests in 2001. That same year fifteen Arts Faculty heads passed a motion expressing concern about the lack of transparency and accountability in the establishment of two commercial enterprises at Melbourne: Melbourne University Private and Universitas 21. Despite these protests, Gilbert is not an unpopular vice-chancellor with many staff because he does not interfere with the academic heartland. He has not restructured the university and has done little to interrupt its daily running. One academic commented in regard to Universitas 21 that the 'University of Melbourne is simply selling its brand name. But because this is far removed from the day-to-day life of academics here, it is unlikely to raise a stir.'[2]

In 2001, Murdoch's vice-chancellor received no-confidence votes from the student guild, the academic staff and the general staff unions. Despite his unpopularity on campus, Schwartz managed to operate in the business world with some commercial acumen and to restructure his university into a commercial enterprise and a much more managerial institution.

At Monash, some academics praised the leadership of Robinson while others were wary of it. One administrator expressed admiration for Robinson and felt he was not micromanaging the institution as was occurring at other Australian universities.[3] However, a pertinent comment was made by one Arts staff member who regretted the current direction of the university:

The commercialization of Monash and the rapid growth of managerialism have created a university where the conditions that created that reputation can no longer be sustained. What will take the place of the educational integrity that created this university is open to speculation but corporate entities are not in the business of providing for the public good or the pursuit of knowledge for its own sake. They are in the business of creating processes which maximize profit.[4]

It is important to note that some academics and administrators at these universities are happy to see their universities become more entrepreneurial. There is also opposition within these universities, but it comes mainly from the arts/humanities side of campus and rarely from faculties such as business, IT or engineering. Here staff members are more comfortable with the entrepreneurial push and many welcome the greater independence from government funding this direction may provide.[5]

Of the three, Gilbert remains as a vice-chancellor but is frustrated with the lack of progress of Australian universities. Light, interviewing Gilbert in 2002, sees him as leading the charge in reforming Australian universities, which he feels are falling behind those in the rest of the world. According to Light, 'He [Gilbert] regrets the widespread ignorance of the role universities could play in a global knowledge revolution' (Light, 2002, pp. 19–20). Each of the three vice-chancellors has utilized all four of Sklair's strategies. Beginning with Sklair's criterion of a global vision, I examine how they positioned their universities to be global players and some of the problems they encountered.

GLOBAL VISION

Universities pride themselves on developing mission statements that accept the challenge of globalization. Sklair suggests that 'A globalizing corporation needs a global vision precisely because it is in the process of denationalizing, redefining its ties to its place of birth, and forging new ties with its global markets and partners' (2001, p. 256). One of the expressions of a global vision that Sklair identifies is the desire to improve the organization. 'The corporation has a vision of being better-organized to fulfil its destiny of global success' (2001, p. 257).

Gilbert established Melbourne University Private (MUP) in 1998 as part of his vision of bringing greater financial independence to Melbourne University. MUP was set up amid predictions that it would dominate the $250 million University Square development, enrol 2,800 fee-paying students and generate billions of dollars of economic activity. It now occupies one floor of one building at University Square. MUP lost millions of dollars and enrolled only 101 fee-paying students. It has now shifted to providing accredited training to commercial clients. It was to recruit academic staff, including professorial appointments. There are now no separate schools or academic staff and it did not attract equity partners.[6]

In 2001, the Victorian State Government asked Gregor Ramsey, former Director-General of Education in New South Wales, to review the university. Dr Ramsey describes MUP as a bold experiment, stating: 'It is not like any other university, not only in Australia, but also in the rest of the world' (Ramsey, 2001, p. 18). It has only four academic areas: leadership and management, international communications and management, energy and environment, and telecommunications, multimedia and IT, developed to appeal to both private and public enterprises. Ramsey notes that they are not the traditional academic areas used to structure a normal university and that 'the entity which now exists is different in scope and function from the one originally given conditional approval to operate as a university' (Kosky, 2002, p. 3). He also describes the university as little more than the commercial arm of the University of Melbourne. At the same time, he encourages the idea of reconceptualizing the notion of a university to include one like MUP that is not set up along 'normal' university lines.

The government of Victoria was not as innovative in its conception of a university and decided it would give the university until 2001 to establish a 'more traditional' notion of a research profile. In the government's view 'client-driven' research alone is not sufficient to satisfy the broad research required of a university. Post-Compulsory Education Minister Lynne Kosky issued an ultimatum to Alan Gilbert: 'conduct academic research at MUP or stop calling it a university.' She could not accept the suggestion by the university that work for corporate clients should be considered research. 'Pure research is about free thinking,' she said. 'As soon as you say research should be demand-driven, you're talking about control of the sort of research that can occur' (cited in Ketchell, 2002).

According to Senator Kim Carr, the opposition spokesman on higher education, 'MUP is a dangerous parasite, an attempt by the vice-chancellor, Alan Gilbert, to get around the rules, to turn the university into a business, while trading on the prestige of the old campus'. The CEO of MUP, David Lloyd, accuses the Victorian government and people sharing Carr's sentiments of trying to destroy the educational experiment, claiming, 'It's the dead hand of socialism reaching up to throttle the future' (Shand, 2002, p. 22).

During the period 1996–2001, Schwartz, tried to transform Murdoch University into a business. In 1996, he issued his vision statement, *Preparing the University for the Twenty-first Century*. Under a heading in the document, 'Make productivity gains and manage strategically', the main actions included collaborating more closely with other universities (from cooperation to mergers) and restructuring to improve management, increase efficiency and free up resources for core functions. New executive deans were to be appointed and made more accountable to management and more distant from academic staff. The 1999 Murdoch's Senate vision statement identified the university's Four Pillars, which were significant for their lack of attention to research or teaching. The pillars supporting the university were:

- develop market attractiveness
- diversify income streams
- build on management efficiency and effectiveness
- create an entrepreneurial culture.

WORLD BEST PRACTICE

Australian universities adopted managerial practices in the area of accountability, drawing on 'world best practices' such as total quality management and benchmarking to develop a culture based on performance indicators. Sklair (2001) suggests that another strategy used by the transnational capitalist class is looking for 'world best practice' (WBP). Along with the quality movement, another practice drawn from business is that of mergers and alliances, and these are penetrating higher education at a fast rate. Cunningham et al. note, 'one of the major observations to be made in relation to the business of education is the hectic activity in seeking partnerships, alliances, outsourcing of services and "content", particularly between educational providers and technology companies' (2000, p. 83).

Universitas 21 is an example of just such an alliance of universities in ten countries, including Australia, China, Canada and the United Kingdom, to provide on-line courses. This is another of Gilbert's initiatives and he is the chair of the U21global board. Melbourne is the largest institutional contributor, having committed US$5m in the first instance, with at least a further $3m in the pipeline. This network, in partnership with Thomson, a Canadian-based publishing giant, will launch Internet University U21global in 2003. Universitas 21 was incorporated in Guernsey, a well-known tax haven. Then in September 2001, U21global was registered in

Singapore, where the activities of trade unions are highly circumscribed. The joint venture capital between the partners is said to be S$90 million (US$51.8 million).

Gilbert confidently asserts the academic integrity and commercial viability of the new venture in words that speak more to the profit motive than to its educational quality:

The fundamental business architecture, brand value and market demand are right, and ... Thomson is a superb partner, with the resources, skills, experience, infrastructure and focus in on-line learning to leverage the brand value accreditation capability of Universitas 21 (Allport, 2001, p. 26)

Academic unions are concerned about the nature of the deal and the fact that there are no plans to include staff in any of the governance structures of the new global university. In 2001, the National Tertiary Education Union (NTEU) in Australia, the Association of University Teachers (AUT) in the United Kingdom and academic unions in New Zealand, Europe and North America called on Universitas 21 to postpone its on-line partnership with Thomson until all academic and employment issues were resolved. Their chief concern was the contracting-out of course content and assessment to Thomson. Three universities, Peking University, the University of Toronto and the University of Michigan, declined to take part in the on-line course offerings. The academic unions object to the commercialization of universities. 'They are concerned that their institutions are investing pots of money into a venture that has no guarantee of commercial success, that has an unproven business model, and that the respect given to their degrees might be diminished if the venture fails' (Hodges, 2002).

Carolyn Allport, NTEU National President, writes about her concerns with U21:

The U21 venture raises important issues about the new models of global delivery and brings into focus the sharp end of the corporatisation of higher education. Under the proposed deal, Thomson Corporation will be responsible for course design, content development, testing and assessment and student database management and translation. The universities will license their 'brand names', receiving money for allowing the crests of their institutions to be used by the new international institution. The universities are not selling their courses; rather it is their reputation that seems up for sale (Allport, 2001, p. 24).

This for-profit venture will derive money from the sale of each institution's brand name and not from the sale of courses. The nature of the work means that there will be a separation of course design and curriculum development from the learning and assessment processes. There is also no guarantee that any of this work will be done by academics at the participating institutions.

FOREIGN DIRECT INVESTMENT

Universities are increasingly investing overseas to gain profit from private campuses. U21global is an example of this type of foreign direct investment (FDI). Sklair argues that there is a connection between FDI and globalization: 'Globalization was necessary to increase shareholder value and foreign direct investment was the strategy through which it was most successfully accomplished for most companies' (2001, p. 84). He also notes that since the 1970s it has become easier for TNCs to invest in almost every country in the world.

Another example of FDI in higher education is the injection of capital from overseas students into the economies of countries like Australia, Canada, the United Kingdom and the United States. Taking Australia as an example, the growth in international students doubled in five years from 1994 to 1998 (41,244 to 84,304). Despite the Asian meltdown in the years 1997–1999, the figures have only slightly decelerated but the growth is still there (Smart and Ang, 1999). In 2001 there were 112,342 international students representing 15.5 per cent of students in Australian universities (Department of Education, Science and Training, 2002).[7] It is interesting to note that Australian off-shore campuses are growing faster than on-campus international student enrolments: from 1997–1998 growth in on-campus international students was 7 per cent while growth in off-shore numbers was 41 per cent (Western Australian Technology and Industry Advisory Council, 2000). These campuses can be identified as foreign direct investment even more clearly than overseas students studying in Australia.

Monash University leads the way in Australia in terms of creating a global university. Its vision is to have a matrix of campuses with nodes in an educational network that spans the globe. It currently has eight campuses, including one in Malaysia and one in South Africa. In addition, it has centres in London and Prato, Italy, and college programmes in China, including in Hong Kong. Partnerships with universities span the globe as well. The university describes itself and its future in a document entitled *Leading the Way: Monash 2020*.

The emerging vision for *Monash 2020* is of a self-reliant, broad-based, global university. Monash is at once international and Australian. And like modern Australia, Monash has embraced the challenges and opportunities of globalization. The most successful of these broad-based universities of the future will be those that can operate simultaneously within nations and globally, and can offer their students and other clients a combination of high-quality campus-based opportunities and technology-assisted distance learning. Monash will develop a global network of campuses, all of which will offer students a gateway to the world. High-quality students and staff will be attracted to Monash to be part of a university with global visibility, global facilities and global standing (Monash University, 2002).

Monash expects to build its network slowly and not necessarily to turn a profit in the short term. It is achieving considerable success with its Malaysian campus. This was established in February 1998 with 350 students. By mid-2001, it had 1,500 students and is now considering a purpose-built campus with a longer-term capacity of up to 8,000 students. However, it has not been clear sailing for Monash University. One problem that emerged with its South African campus, launched in October 2000, was that the South African government refused to allow the institution to be called a university and it had to be renamed simply Monash South Africa.

CORPORATE CITIZENSHIP

Modelled on companies, universities now think of themselves as corporate citizens. Sklair gives this description of corporate citizenship:

With economic globalization and changing local conditions, business leaders are called upon to wrestle with complex issues that affect not only their shareholders, employees and customers but also the quality of life in local communities, our environment and people and countries throughout the world (Sklair, 2001, p. 159).

This suggests that business leaders are interested in more than the bottom line, and even consider the quality of life in their communities.

Under Schwartz, Murdoch University adopted a corporate agenda and portrayed itself as a corporate citizen. As with many new CEOs, Schwartz developed a new logo and motto for his corporate image of the university. In a document describing the university, he referred to it as a corporate citizen in the community. At the same time, he planned to lease campus land for a petrol station (with three already within a few kilometres of the university) and a fast food outlet (with several near by). He also signed a contract with a mobile phone company to build a tower near the childcare centre. Along with petitions and protests from staff and students, a number of community meetings were held to protest against these developments. As a result, the university did not proceed with the mobile tower, the petrol station, or the fast food outlet. However, it leased land for three commercial projects: Murdoch College, St. Ives Retirement Home and Lakeview Apartments. Although there was opposition to a number of the vice-chancellor's entrepreneurial initiatives and to the use of the words, 'corporate citizen', he succeeded in transforming the university into a corporate entity.

GLOBALIZATION AND GLOBAL UNIVERSITIES: AN ASSESSMENT

There is no doubt that, in the current climate, Australian universities are struggling to survive financially. The government has turned its back on universities, ignoring their pleas for increased funding and stating that there is no crisis in Australian universities. In addition the current Education Minister, Brendan Nelson, continues to target academic staff in his review of higher education. He wants universities to develop a more efficient workforce, one that is 'more supple, sassier and commercially-minded' (Richardson, 2002, p. 2). The current government believes in greater deregulation of the system and more managerial solutions to the universities' problems. However, there are certainly other models that could be considered to lead these universities in a direction that is less managerial and less reliant on business practices while still ensuring that they do not go bankrupt.

These three vice-chancellors acted as global players, believing that they could position their universities to best compete on the global stage. This was not easy. Each made bold decisions. They met resistance every step of the way. This was most clearly seen in the cases of Melbourne and Murdoch. There was also unease at Monash over the extension of the university to so many locations and its move towards greater managerialism.

The vice-chancellors had clear agendas and were willing to take risks to be global players. In the end, they all brought a more entrepreneurial style of management to their universities. Management theory can be useful to universities if embedded in democratic collegiality, a representative form of collegiality that encourages dialogue about academic issues and an inclusive decision-making process (see Currie, 1999). This did not occur, as 'new management' was overlaid on patriarchal collegiality, based on the old boys' network and favouritism. As a result, an aggressive, patriarchal managerialism has emerged in most Australian universities, increasing stress and mistrust among staff (Currie et al., 2002). This is not a healthy context for managers or workers.

In the ideal rhetoric of the mission statements of these universities, there are many benefits to be gained from investing in overseas campuses and developing alliances with 'brand name' universities in other countries. In fact, these global practices could benefit other countries as well as Australia, especially if they follow their stated objectives. For example, *Monash 2020* states that the university overseas campuses should be integrated into the culture of the country and each university should contribute to 'the well-being and development of the country in which it is located' (Monash University, 2002). Being civic-minded requires a different kind of citizenship, one centred on the public interest. The public interest value of universities is one of the crucial losses that come with the privatization of universities. It is no doubt true that global universities can compete better in the productivity and profit stakes, but are they losing a certain type of generosity towards the community.

CONCLUSION

There is growing support for alternative visions after 9/11 and increasing concerns about the impact of globalization on communities and the inequities created by relying on a free market ideology. These concerns are evident if we consider the political trajectory of globalization over the past two decades. In the 1980s and early 1990s, it did not seem to matter much whether an ostensibly left- or right-oriented government was in power in most Anglo-American countries. These governments ushered in changes that led to acceptance of the global practices of privatization, marketization, and new managerialism. All made radical changes to the way universities were organized and to the lives of academic workers. Currently, there are concerns about whether the move to the New Right has gone too far, with too great a loss to public services. For example, Henderson (2001) reports that privatization in Australia delivered little improvement to the financial performance of most government businesses. Even in the United States, where the efficacy of the market is most trusted, there are questions raised about privatization and deregulation. After the September 11 attacks, US politicians replaced private providers of airport security systems with federally-hired screeners. In Dallas, school trustees voted to end their contract with Edison Schools, the largest for-profit school chain in the United States, because test scores were not good enough to justify their fees (*Newsweek*, 2 September 2002, p. 10). Even Nobel Prize-winning economist, former Chief Economist of the World Bank, Joseph Stiglitz (2002), argues for changes to IMF and World Bank policies and explains the shortcomings of current global economic policies.

In a comprehensive review of the empirical work on privatization, Birdsall and Nellis conclude, 'At least initially, and on average, privatization has worsened wealth distribution (highly likely) and income distribution (likely)' (2002, p. 18). A number of Asian countries are eschewing the privatization route and instead funding their universities at a higher rate.

Despite these setbacks in the ideology of neo-liberal globalization, global forces will not disappear. Universities will continue to be challenged by a changing world that is becoming more integrated with each new advance in communications technology. The borderless world is a reality in many aspects of our lives and will become more so in the future. The more corporate universities will take advantage of this borderless world.

Academics, however, are often repulsed by the corporatization of universities. This is exemplified by the number of academics leaving Australian universities, citing specifically the increasing commercialization of their universities. A lead story in *The Australian* in 2002 captured the feelings of two of the prominent academics, one leaving Melbourne and the other Monash. Simon During, accepting a position at Johns Hopkins, stated: 'The pressure to make money for universities has almost become the overriding part of the academic's brief. As a result the intellectual life at Australian universities has been significantly weakened' (Madden, 2002, p. 31). A week later two more humanities professors left for posts in American universities, stating that they had lost faith in the Australian university system. One was from Monash and he cited a catalogue of reasons for leaving the university, focusing on the devaluing of excellence and originality that had been prized by Monash in the past.

The search for profits risks the loss of essential university values, developing thoughtful citizens and creating a scholarly community based on trust. These values can exist in global universities. However, they are more likely to be found in universities that are democratically-collegial, publicly-funded and community-oriented rather than in managerial universities established to make a profit. We must cherish these values and guard against their disappearance in the global universities we create.

NOTES

1. The past tense is used for Schwartz and Robinson because they resigned from their positions in Australian universities in 2001 and 2002 respectively.
2. Personal e-mail communication, Melbourne academic, 30 August 2002.
3. Personal e-mail communication, Monash administrator and former Murdoch academic, 29 August 2002.
4. Personal e-mail communication, Monash staff member, 30 August 2002.
5. Personal e-mail communication, Monash academic and former Melbourne academic, 25 September 2002.
6. MUP merged with the successful Hawthorn English Language Center and now makes a profit.
7. This percentage contrasts with the United States where international students comprised only 3.8 per cent of tertiary enrolments in the 1999/2000 academic year (NAFSA, 2001).

BIBLIOGRAPHY

Allport, C. 2001. Educating and Organizing Globally: Perspectives on the Internet and Higher Education. *Australian Universities' Review*, Vol. 44, Nos. 1–2, pp. 21–6.

Bachelard, M. 2001. From Schoolboy Bullies to Bosses Behaving Badly. *The Australian*, 30 May, p. 13.

Birdsall, N. and Nellis, J. 2002. Winners and Losers: Assessing the Distributional Impact of Privatization. Working Paper No. 6, May. Washington, D.C., Center for Global Development.

Cunningham, S., Ryan, Y., Tapsall, S., Stedman, L., Bagdon, K., Flew, T. and Coaldrake, P. 2000. *The Business of Borderless Education.* Canberra, DETYA's Evaluations and Investigations Programme.

Currie, J. 1999. *Alternative Responses to Globalization Practices in Universities: The Value of Democracy.* Paper presented at the Conference on Re-Organizing Knowledge: Transforming Institutions, Knowing, Knowledge and the University in the Twenty-first Century, University of Massachusetts, Amherst, 17–19 September.

Currie, J., DeAngelis, R., de Boer, H., Huisman, J., and Lacotte, C. 2002. *Global Practices and University Responses: European and Anglo-American Differences.* Westport, Conn., Greenwood Press.

Currie, J., Thiele, B., and Harris, T. 2002. *Gendered Universities in Globalized Economies: Power, Careers and Sacrifices.* Lanham, Md., Lexington.

Department of Education, Science, and Training. 2002. Statistics Relating to Higher Education 2001. Australian Commonwealth Government, Canberra. Retrieved 1 August 2002 from: www.det.govau/highered/statinfo.html.

Economist. 2001. Is Globalization Doomed? 29 September, p. 13.

Hall, P. A.; Soskice, D. 2001. *Varieties of Capitalism.* Oxford, Oxford University Press.

Henderson, I. 2001. Little to Show for Reforms. *The Australian*, 12 June, p. 10.

Hodges, L. 2002. Higher Education: Why Dons Won't be Logging on Today. The Association of University Teachers is Voting to Boycott On-line Courses run by an Elite Group of Universities Around the World. *The Independent* (United Kingdom), 25 April.

Ketchell, M. 2002. Melbourne Uni Private Gets Research Ultimatum. *The Age*, 7 February. Retrieved 14 February 2002 from: ww.theage.comm.au/news/state/2002/02/07.

Kosky, L. 2002. Review of Melbourne University Private Ministerial Response. Victorian Minister for Post-Compulsory Education Training and Employment and Minister for Finance, February.

Light, D. 2002. University Challenge. *The Bulletin*, 9 April, pp. 18–23.

Madden, J. 2002. How Simon Got his Grove Back. *The Australian*, 3 July, p. 31.

Monash University. 2002. Global Development. Retrieved 9 August 2002 from: www.monash.edu.au/intoff/globaldevelopment/framework/campuses.html.

NAFSA: Association of International Educators. 2001. Public Policy/data on International Education. Retrieved June 2001 from: www.nafsa.org/content/PublicPolicy/DataonInternationalEducation/data.htm.

Ramsey, G. 2001. The Report of a Review of Melbourne University Private Limited for the Minister for Post Compulsory Education, Training and Employment, December.

Richardson, J. 2002. Performance Pay Plan for University Staff. *The Australian*, 15 August, p. 2.

Shand, A. 2002. Who's afraid of Melbourne University Private? *The Weekend Australian Financial Review*, 1–2 June, p. 22-23.

Sklair, L. 2001. *The Transnational Capitalist Class*. Oxford, Blackwell.

Smart, D. and Ang, G. 1999. The Impact of the Asian Economic Meltdown on WA Educational Institutions 1997–1999. In: D. Davis and A. Olsen, *International Education: The Professional Edge*, pp. 117–34. Canberra: IDP Education Australia.

Stiglitz, J. E. 2002. *Globalization and Its Discontents*. New York, W. W. Norton.

Surowiecki, J. 2001. The Financial Page: Bad Company. *The New Yorker*, 12 March, p. 46.

Western Australian Technology and Industry Advisory Council. 2000. *Export of Western Australian Education & Training Constraints and Opportunities*. Perth, Western Australian Technology and Industry Advisery Council.

13. New Models for Higher Education: Creating an Adult-Centred Institution

Craig D. Swenson

AN ERA OF CHANGE

We are witnesses to a unique era of human history during which global forces are combining to produce rapid and profound change on a heretofore unknown scale. A sense of disequilibrium pervades every aspect of our lives and is placing great stress on society's fundamental institutions. None of our systems are spared, including our global system of higher education.

Academicians face a unique dilemma. By profession, we study the changes and forces for change in society and its institutions. We measure, evaluate and predict these changes and their ramifications to other areas of life and culture. We propose interventions that will deal with the dislocations and chaos our organizations face. Ironically, many of us seem to believe that our own educational institutions and networks of institutions should remain static – as if that were even a possibility – as if there were a platonic form for colleges and universities to which we should be attempting to conform. Like it or not, of course, higher education is as subject to the aforementioned forces as any other societal entity.

As with every other type of institution, we know that new structural forms will appear in higher education, the result of varied combinations of economic, demographic, cultural and technological forces. Some of these will disappear as quickly as they arose. Others, having met some basic societal need, will survive and even displace revered but obsolete structures that have been unable to adapt. This is not to suggest that traditional colleges and universities will disappear. It is most likely that a variety of institutional types will exist and prosper. But some will fail and all will invariably be changed by these forces. This chapter describes one institutional variation, the University of Phoenix, which arose in the United States over the past quarter century – the result of the forces adumbrated above.

CREATING AN 'ADULT-CENTRED' UNIVERSITY

In 1976, the leading-edge members of the baby-boom generation were just turning 30. That same year saw the introduction of the first personal computer, the Apple I, an event that signalled the birth of a new economic system through which intellectual capital would eventually supplant industrial might as the dominant global economic force. These milestones also marked the beginning of a sea change in American higher education, though many (perhaps even most) within that system did not recognize it at the time.

Considered together, these phenomena suggested that the jobs that would make up the workforce of the future were only just beginning to be created or imagined. In order to fill those jobs, the bulk of the new workforce would require different, higher-level knowledge and skills than those needed in a manufacturing economy. At the same time, the largest-ever age cohort of the population, working adults, would be going through the stages of life during which they would be most affected by the coming economic dislocation and would need advanced education to adapt to these changes.

It was in this historical context in 1976, that Dr John Sperling, a Cambridge-educated economist and professor-turned-entrepreneur, founded University of Phoenix. Sperling anticipated the confluence of technological, economic and demographic forces that would in a very short time herald the return of ever-larger numbers of working adults to formal higher education.

Over the course of the past quarter-century, University of Phoenix has become the largest private university in the United States, with a current enrolment of nearly 140,000. It operates campus locations where face-to-face instruction is provided in twenty-six states, Puerto Rico, British Columbia and Rotterdam in the Netherlands. It also currently enrols nearly 50,000 in its Online Campus, including representatives from forty different countries. The university attributes its growth to an unwavering focus on serving its unique student population, including the creation of a teaching–learning model designed specifically for working adults. It has been equally devoted to creating an organizational culture in which innovation and continuous improvement are core values. The university's future includes plans for international expansion, primarily through its Online Campus.

Many of the same dynamics seen in the United States are also evident in other areas of the world. Increasingly, global economic development will depend not only on educating young people to take their places as citizens and preparing them to earn living wages, but also on the revitalization of the existing population of working adults through the practices of lifelong learning. Responding to global economic competition will require a more rapid retooling of a country's work force than waiting for new workers to enter will allow. Thus, institutions like University of Phoenix may offer lessons about structuring higher education for non-traditional students.

BEGINNINGS

In the early 1970s, at San Jose State University in San Jose, California, Sperling and several associates conducted field-based research in adult education. The focus of the research was to explore teaching–learning systems for the delivery of educational programmes and services to working adult students who wished to complete or further their education in ways that complemented both their experience and current professional responsibilities.

At that time colleges and universities were organized primarily around serving the needs of the 18–22-year-old undergraduate student. That is not at all surprising, given that the large majority of those enrolled were residential students of traditional college age, just out of high school. According to Sperling, working adult students were invisible on the traditional campus and were treated as second-class citizens:

Other than holding classes at night (and many universities did not even do this), no efforts were made to accommodate their needs. No university offices or bookstores were open at night. Students had to leave work during the day to enrol, register for classes, buy books or consult with their instructors and advisers. Classes were held two or three nights per week and parking was at the periphery of a large campus. The consequence, according to Dr Sperling, was that most working adult students were unable to finish a four-year programme in less than eight years, or a two-year programme in less than four years (Tucker, 1996, p. 5).

Sperling's research convinced him not only that working adult students were interested in furthering their educational goals but also that they differed from their younger counterparts in significant ways. He saw a growing need for institutions sensitive to and designed around the learning characteristics and life situations of the working adult population. He suggested how these institutions could pioneer new approaches to curricular and programme design, teaching methods and student services.

These beliefs eventually resulted in the creation of University of Phoenix, and they continue to this day to inspire the University's mission, purposes and strategies. As an institution, University of Phoenix is unique in its single-minded commitment to the educational needs of working adults. This focus informs the University's teaching and learning model, approach to designing and providing student services, and academic and administrative structure. It also guides the institution as it plans and prepares to meet the needs of working adult students.

A UNIQUE MISSION

The University's Statement of Mission and Purposes focuses clearly on student learning and identifies that focus as the vehicle through which broader institutional goals will be pursued. It also emphasizes innovation, convenience, continuous improvement, and service quality as essential to the achievement of the University's mission.

The mission of University of Phoenix is to educate working adults to develop the knowledge and skills that will enable them to achieve their professional goals, improve the productivity of their organizations, and provide leadership and service to their communities.

The purposes are:

- To facilitate cognitive and affective student learning – knowledge, skills and values – and to promote use of that knowledge in the student's work place.
- To develop competence in communication, critical thinking, collaboration and information utilization, together with a commitment to lifelong learning for enhancement of students' opportunities for career success.
- To provide instruction that bridges the gap between theory and practice through faculty members who bring to their classrooms not only advanced academic preparation, but also the skills that come from the current practice of their professions.

- To use technology to create effective modes and means of instruction that expand access to learning resources and that enhance collaboration and communication for improved student learning.
- To assess student learning and use assessment data to improve the teaching–learning system, curriculum, instruction, learning resources, counselling and student services.
- To be organized as a for-profit institution in order to foster a spirit of innovation that focuses on providing academic quality, service, excellence, and convenience to the working adult.
- To generate the financial resources necessary to support the university's mission.

A TEACHING–LEARNING MODEL FOR WORKING ADULTS

Because University of Phoenix exists to serve the working adult population, the University's teaching–learning model is grounded in the theoretical and empirical literature of adult learning and cognitive psychology, and employs best practice from the adult education literature. Its essential features are described below

Active learning
The model is based first on the assumption that the learner's active involvement in the learning process is essential to good practice. Creating instruction that utilizes the affective domain enables the adult learner to connect more extensively with the cognitive domain. Thus, University of Phoenix classrooms are intended to be dynamic learning spaces. Instructors are expected to serve as facilitators of learning who manage the learning process by engaging learners in a variety of activities (lectures being but one) that lead students to an understanding of course content and the development of academic and professional competence. By involving students in a variety of learning activities, respect is demonstrated for diverse ways of learning and knowing. Interaction and participation in classes and learning teams is expected. While there are certainly didactic elements in every course, these are augmented and enhanced by student participation through discussion, debate, reflection and application.

A learning environment based on collaboration
The effectiveness of cooperation and collaboration in enhancing learning is well and widely documented. Structures that encourage and facilitate

collaboration are central to the teaching–learning model. Working adults generally come to formal learning activities with significantly greater life and work experience than their younger counterparts. This means that learners themselves can be invaluable resources in enhancing their own and others' learning. Traditional pedagogy emphasizes a top-down, vertical transfer of information. Adult students with rich and varied experience find benefit in instructional practices that encourage collaboration. This adds a robust 'horizontal' dimension to the learning exchange as adult students teach and learn from one another.

A unique programme format

University of Phoenix does not operate according to a traditional academic calendar. New student cohorts can begin at any time and classes are held throughout the year without traditional quarter or semester breaks. Typically, graduate courses at University of Phoenix meet for six consecutive weeks and undergraduate courses meet for five weeks. When a course ends, the next course usually begins the following week. This intensive calendar allows adult students to achieve their educational goals in a more time-efficient manner.

The University's low student–faculty ratio, with class sizes that average thirteen students, facilitates active learning and collaboration, encourages time-on-task and fosters high student–faculty interaction. As a rule, students take only one course at a time. This allows focus on one subject. This structure enhances learning and helps students balance ongoing professional and personal responsibilities.

- *On-campus instruction.* During a typical on-campus course, students participate in two instructional activities each week: a four-hour workshop facilitated by the faculty member, and a 4–5 hour learning team session. Learning teams are intact groups of from three to five students drawn from within the larger cohort. Learning teams foster students' abilities to collaborate: a competency expected of employees in information age organizations and one of the University's primary learning goals. Faculty members closely monitor the learning team activities, outcomes and processes through review of learning team logs and charters.
- *Online Campus instruction.* Students who complete their academic programmes through the Online Campus participate in an asynchronous electronic conferencing format that allows them to participate at the

times and places that work best for them within required timeframes. The University is also developing a new instructional format called FlexNet: a hybrid delivery method that blends the campus and on-line modalities.

An emphasis on application and relevance

There is wide agreement in the literature that adults learn best when bridges are built between new knowledge and the learner's experience. Practices that encourage reflection and application are based on the recognition that a learner's experience provides a context through which he or she is more able to construct meaning from new information. It also makes learning relevant to the learners, increasing affective connection with subject matter and the likelihood that they will respond with a deep versus surface approach to learning. In University of Phoenix courses, students' past experiences and current circumstances are interwoven with subject matter in class discussions as well as in individual and learning team assignments. Students very often say they are able to apply at work the next day what they learned in class the night before.

Building professional competence

The University's faculty leadership has established five broad 'learning goals' that guide curriculum development, instruction, learning assessment, and programme evaluation and improvement. The first of these goals, *Professional Competence and Values*, relates to the discipline-specific course and programme content. University of Phoenix wants its graduates to attain levels of theoretical and practical disciplinary knowledge appropriate to the levels of degrees or credentials they are earning (bachelor, master, or doctoral level). The remaining four goals relate to the development of competence in essential intellectual and social processes that will enable graduates to practise their professions successfully. They are *Critical Thinking and Problem-Solving, Communication, Information Utilization* and *Collaboration*.

OTHER FEATURES OF THE MODEL

Convenience of time and place

University of Phoenix classroom programmes are offered at times and in places that are convenient for working adults. Classes are held primarily in the evening and at weekends when working adults are most likely to need access. Wherever possible, campuses and learning centres are located at strategic locations near major freeways and thoroughfares that permit convenient access. Campus facilities, including both instructional and administrative space, are generally housed in Class A or equivalent space, and are established under long-term leases of from five to ten years. This allows the institution to respond with flexibility to shifts in population.

Adult-friendly student services

University of Phoenix has found that adult students tend to hold higher expectations of student services than do their younger counterparts. These students expect from the University the same levels of attention and convenience they expect from any other service provider. Increasingly, this implies 24×7 access to student services. Services are provided through electronic or telephone access as much as possible, although person-to-person service is always available. For example, rather than requiring students to drive to a campus bookstore, texts and course materials are ordered via the Internet or by toll-free telephone and delivered directly to the student's home.

Students attending University of Phoenix on-line courses enjoy the same commitment to student service as campus students. Through years of experience in on-line education, the University has learned that an even greater investment in the quality and availability of student services must be made to ensure that students who attend courses at a distance persist and succeed. The Online Campus is structured around the particular needs and abilities of the kinds of students who select distributed learning as their preferred method.

THE UNIVERSITY'S FACULTY

From the founding of University of Phoenix to the present day perhaps the greatest institutional challenge has been to build innovative structures that support the university's unique mission. The result is a model that assures that essential roles performed by the faculty in any teaching university are also fulfilled at University of Phoenix, though sometimes in a different fashion. To a degree, this model represents what has come to be referred to as an unbundled or disaggregated approach.

Why a different faculty model?

Based on his initial field-based research in the early 1970s, the university's founder, Dr John Sperling, concluded that a classroom full of adults enrolled in professional education is a qualitatively distinct place from one filled with 18–22-year-olds. He found that adult students brought very different expectations regarding the kind of instruction they receive than did his younger students in a traditional setting. According to recent research by the College Board (Aslanian, 2001, p.16) more than 80 per cent of adults who return for advanced education do so because of a desire to advance in their professions and careers. That percentage is up from 70 per cent just a decade ago.

From an instructional standpoint, the most significant issue relates to the resulting expectation that instruction will be of immediate practical relevance. This does not mean that working adults do not recognize a need for or desire an understanding of the theory of a discipline – especially when they come to understand how a grasp of theory helps them in situations and events in the professional setting and enables them to predict the consequences of interventions. They do expect, however, that the theory will be taught in the context of practice and application. As a result, they often display a lower degree of patience for instructors who are not equipped by experience to do this. This is significant because working adults, having consciously chosen to pursue education, often at significant personal and financial cost, are more likely to vote with their feet and pocketbooks. This should not be taken to indicate that adult students want their education to be easy: they readily grasp that rigour and credibility are related. It has been the University's experience that in order to attract and retain adult students, format and instruction must be consistent with their self-perceived needs as well as the educational needs an institution identifies for them.

John Sperling discovered that the faculty members favoured by these students, and those from whom they reported learning more, brought to the classroom not only advanced academic preparation in a field but also the significant practical professional experience that facilitated the marriage of theory and practice. He also noted, through his comparison of learning outcomes, that there was no degradation of results. He ultimately concluded that an institution whose sole mission was to serve working adults could craft an innovative model that used these insights to its advantage and set out to do so.

Implications of the faculty model: faculty roles

Outcomes data suggest that a teaching faculty comprised predominantly of professional practitioners is an effective way to educate working adults. Adopting this model has required, however, that University of Phoenix

The course module is not set in stone, however. Latitude is given to the teaching faculty member to exercise academic judgement. He or she may choose to enhance or change assignments and design learning activities not included in the teaching notes. The basic requirement is that the course must be taught and assessed to the objectives identified by the faculty team at the appropriate academic level.

Teaching

As mentioned previously, the University practises a collaborative, facilitative instructional model. For this reason, and because the majority of University of Phoenix instructors are not traditional full-time faculty members for whom teaching is a primary occupation, it is incumbent on the University to ensure that those appointed to the faculty can demonstrate the ability or potential to teach effectively in this environment.

To this end, all faculty candidates participate in a rigorous screening and assessment process. It begins with a resume or curriculum vitae review to ensure that they meet the basic requirements for approval, which include a graduate degree from a regionally accredited institution and at least five years of employment in their field – two of which must have occurred subsequent to completion of a master's degree. Practitioner faculty candidates must also be currently employed in the discipline in which they teach. The next step is a 'content interview' with an experienced faculty member from the candidate's discipline. The purpose is to ensure that candidates bring the breadth, depth and current knowledge of the content area in which they will be teaching.

Candidates are then invited to demonstrate their ability to facilitate learning in an assessment experience during which candidates are observed and evaluated by senior faculty members. In addition, all new faculty members complete extensive training as part of the Faculty Certification Process: a four-session course augmented by Web- and paper-based readings and training modules. This experience is designed to model appropriate facilitation practice at the University and provides additional content and training in areas such as adult learning theory and practice, facilitation skills, learning team administration, grading, evaluation, assessment, governance and administrative procedures, and the University library. The Faculty Certification module was developed by a team of full-time faculty members from four of the seven regions across the University, two representatives from central administration, academic affairs and an instructional design consultant

Those who successfully complete this process then apply for approval to teach specific courses offered by the University. The Dean or his/her designee judge the member's academic and professional experience specific to the faculty course approval requirements created for the course. The final step for a new faculty member is participation in a mentorship with an experienced faculty member during the first course he or she teaches.

Ongoing training and development opportunities are made available to the entire faculty through regular faculty training meetings and Web-based training modules. Additionally, faculty members receive a *Faculty Handbook* that includes the Faculty Standards with which faculty members are expected to comply in order to remain in good standing with the University, as well as all pertinent policies, procedures and expectations.

Faculty scholarship

University of Phoenix is a teaching institution whose focus is professional education for working adults. While formal academic research is not a requirement of the practitioner faculty, the University recognizes that an important precursor to fulfilment of the fundamental aspects of our Mission and Purposes related to student learning and development is a faculty that engages appropriately in scholarly activities. In an institution that serves a specialized population and employs a disaggregated or unbundled faculty model, this necessitates a different approach to scholarship than would be found in a traditional setting.

Contrary to perceptions that a faculty comprised so largely of practitioners would not actively engage the 'scholarship of discovery', a recent compilation of scholarship activities of the University's faculty indicates otherwise. The University has recently begun a process of automating its faculty files. This has allowed the aggregation of reports of the academic and professional activities in which the University's faculty is involved and the scholarship produced. The initial results of the survey among full-time faculty suggest that there is significant ongoing scholarship – in all the dimensions described by Boyer – taking place within the faculty.

Additionally, the University's Virtual Community of Scholars is an on-line community that fosters exchange of research ideas and resources among faculty and doctoral students. Faculty chat rooms serve as links for exchange of best practices, both in education and in real world application and trends across disciplines. It is designed to promote scholarship and to provide a forum for the University's faculty to publish their research and learning appropriately. This new endeavour is still in the early stages of development.

INSTITUTIONAL AND OUTCOMES ASSESSMENT: ENSURING CONSISTENT QUALITY

Over the past two decades, University of Phoenix has made significant investments in developing and maintaining institutional research capabilities. These systems measure and evaluate the University's effectiveness in achieving objectives and improving institutional processes. The foundation of the University's evaluation and assessment efforts was laid in the 1980s. This foundation continues to rest on two pillars refined in the early 1990s: the Academic Quality Management System (AQMS), focusing on the performance of educational support systems including faculty, curriculum and student services, and the Adult Learning Outcomes Assessment (ALOA), focusing on the measurement of student learning in both the cognitive and affective domains.

These assessment systems have brought significant public recognition to University of Phoenix over the past decade and the institution has continued innovation in this area through a 'reengineering' of its assessment processes over the past two years.

MAKING A DIFFERENCE IN COMMUNITIES

When University of Phoenix enters a community, it is sometimes perceived as a threat to existing institutions. Initial concerns tend to subside with the realization that the University focuses on a different population segment than most others. Additionally, the resources spent to attract new students stimulate a general interest in higher education and, ultimately, contribute to an overall increase in adult students returning to other institutions as well.

University of Phoenix provides social and economic benefits by helping to meet the educational needs of working adults without adversely affecting the existing higher education system. As a for-profit, adult-centred institution, the University does not draw on states' educational resources, but instead offers economic advantages. Some of these advantages include: a) withdrawal of less federal and state income taxes and local property and sales taxes, returning more to the public treasury than their students take out in the form of grants and below-market federally insured loans; b) access to private capital for funds needed for start-up and/or expansion; and c) operation from leased commercial space that can be designed and built in a matter of months to meet student needs. Perhaps, most importantly, the University contributes to state economies by providing educational opportunities so that working adults can enhance their knowledge and skills and, as a result, continue to be productive citizens.

With the University's emphasis on professional programmes, these are some of the areas where it is making a contribution in the communities it serves:

- A quarter of the University's enrolments during 2001 entered degree programmes where significant national shortages are being reported (information systems and technology, teacher education, health sciences and nursing, counselling and human services).
- Since its establishment in 1976, some 125,000 students have graduated from University of Phoenix. In 2000, more than 25,000 students graduated and continued to be a part of the nation's workforce.
- Nearly 65 per cent of University of Phoenix students who begin two-three- or four-year degree programmes, whether in campus-based or On-line Campus programmes, will complete them, despite the competing interests of work, family and community. This is in contrast to a national graduation rate in the United States of 58 per cent.
- University of Phoenix has demonstrated a significantly higher than average level of participation and graduation by members of minority populations. Fully 40 per cent of University of Phoenix students identify themselves as members of an ethnic minority.
- 65 per cent of the University's candidates for admission come from referrals from satisfied students, alumni and their employers.
- 94 per cent of graduates said they would recommend University of Phoenix to another adult student.
- 43 per cent of graduates reported receiving a promotion since completing their degrees.

For its many adult students, the University's contributions will be life changing. The educational experience provided has helped foster new ways of seeing the world and has improved quality of life; it has contributed to the success of their organizations as they become more effective professionals, thinkers and problem-solvers; and it enables them to make contributions in their communities and to the larger society.

BIBLIOGRAPHY

Aslanian, C. B. 2001. *Adult Students Today.* New York, The College Board.

Boyer, E. L. 1990. *Scholarship Reconsidered: Priorities for the Professoriate.* Princeton, N.J., Carnegie Foundation for the Advancement of Teaching.

Kolb, D. A. and Frey, R. 1975. Toward an Applied Theory of Experiential Learning. In: G. Cooper, *Theories of Group Processes.* New York, John Wiley.

Tucker, R. S. 1996. From the Void: An Interview with John Sperling. *Adult Assessment Forum*, Vol. 6, No. 2, pp. 4–7.

14. Changing Players in a Knowledge Society

Peter Scott

The aim of this contribution to the increasingly urgent – even frenetic – debate about the impact of globalization on higher education is to offer a revisionist, or counter-intuitive, account. The argument presented here is, first, that the institutions most people expect to be the winners in the knowledge society – such as 'virtual' and corporate universities, or global coalitions of research universities, or 'knowledge-brokering' management consultants – may in fact play a peripheral, even subordinate, role; and, second and consequently, that traditional universities should not feel they have no choice but to model themselves on such institutions. In other words, the contrast that is often drawn between this supposed 'new economy' in higher education, associated with GATS (General Agreement on Trade in Services) and ICTs (information and communication technologies) and other neo-liberal paraphernalia, on the one hand, and the academic equivalent of 'smoke-stack industry', in other words traditional academic and scholarly practice, on the other hand, may be profoundly misleading. However, such a revisionist argument does not mean that universities can afford to be complacent, still less that the current character and taxonomy of institutions represents the best of all possible worlds. On the contrary it suggests that universities may need to be even more radical – but in unexpected ways.

The standard account is based on a view that higher education – both teaching and research (although the latter has retained a strategic significance) – is a commodity. Initially the impact of this view on higher education policy was confined to national policy-making as welfare states began to crumble during the 1980s. Private benefits were emphasized instead of public goods as the near-exclusive outcomes of higher education. As a result students, now seen as predominant beneficiaries in terms of enhanced lifetime earnings, were in turn expected to make a direct contribution to the cost of providing that higher education in the form of increased tuition fees. During the 1990s this commodification of higher education extended beyond national frontiers as neo-liberal globalization tightened its grip. The lesson drawn by many political (and university) leaders was that the way forward for higher education was to abandon collectivist public-service public-sector policies and practices and embrace the 'market'; universities must seize the opportunity to become the leading organizations in the burgeoning global knowledge economy. Not to seize this opportunity was to risk marginalization – even, eventually, extinction. The discussion of the impact of globalization on higher education continues to be dominated by this neo-liberal orthodoxy, but it is this orthodoxy (better, ideology) that must be challenged if universities are successfully to embrace the 'world', in all its problematical diversity, rather than simply the global marketplace.

THE UNIVERSITY IN THE KNOWLEDGE SOCIETY

The debate about the impact of globalization on the university is characterized by both urgency and naivety, the former compounding the latter. The urgency is manifest in terms of policy. The fear appears to be that, unless the university reacts and adapts – not tomorrow or even today but yesterday – to the challenges of globalization, it is in danger of becoming an anachronism, an institutional hulk beached on the deserted shores of the nation/welfare state from which the tide of social, economic and cultural development is rapidly receding. The naivety is manifest in terms of concepts and analyses. Too often both globalization and the university are treated as stereotypes, the former (negatively or positively) as a Brave New World of global markets and communications, and the latter as an unproblematic (and, consequently, static?) institution. My starting-point is that this urgency needs to be questioned and this naivety challenged.

   Globalization is more than simply a market-led techno-phenomenon. It is bound up in the larger development of a knowledge society, and also intimately linked to changes in knowledge production. There is a risk that the knowledge society is now such a widely used (over-used?) term that it can mean all things to all people, as is indicated by the plethora of different versions (information society, informational society, network society and so on). However, despite the fecundity and diversity of meanings, it is still used as if it were an entirely unproblematic category. It is important, therefore, to emphasize the instability of, and contradictions inherent in, the idea of a 'knowledge society'. To (over?) simplify, there are three different meanings that can be attached to this idea.

- The first meaning is derived from technological determinism, and focuses on the impact of information and communication technologies – round-the-globe round-the-clock financial markets, global media and brands; in short, the world of CNN and Coca Cola. But this is not just a techno-logical fix. This shift is also reflected in fundamental changes in modes of production: the idea of a post-industrial society. And it extends into the political, and even cultural, domains. As a result, it is argued, older forms of collectivist engagement between citizens and the state have been superseded by direct, even instantaneous, interaction between individual consumers and mass markets. Closely linked with this, of course, is the notion of globalization, the idea that nation states have had their day.
- The second meaning attached to the idea of the 'knowledge society' is derived from geopolitical analyses, which often pick up the globalization theme. The latest, and an intriguing, example is Philip Bobbitt's book *The Shield of Achilles: War, Peace and the Course of History*. He argues that a series of epochal wars have produced fundamental shifts in the characteristics of both states and the world order. According to Bobbitt the 'long war' of 1914 to 1980 – which, incidentally, was 'won' by the 'West' mainly because of its superiority in information systems – has led to the eclipse of the nation state by the market state. His is a rather more subtle version of the triumphalist account offered by Francis Fukuyama ten years ago. Paul Kennedy and others have written in a similar vein.
- The third meaning is rooted in deeper social and cultural analyses. These range from optimistic – and, perhaps, rather mechanistic – accounts of social change such as Manuel Castells' trilogy on the Network Society, *The Information Age*, (which tend to assume that technological determinism is the dominant driver of social and cultural change)· to much more sombre accounts, such as that offered by Ulrich Beck in his *Risk Society*, which emphasize the fragmentation of social meaning and

atomization of individual experience. Closely allied are the gloomy scenarios offered by environmentalists, and even the violent protests against globalization. Also linked, although indirectly, are notions of intellectual volatility – verging at times on the excesses of postmodernism – because grand narratives, over-arching conceptualizations and meta-theories have been made redundant by the 'acceleration' of knowledge and the ability to manipulate massive data-sets (Lyotard, 1984).

It is not possible to go more deeply into these rival meanings of the knowledge society in a paper concerned with the impact of globalization on the university. But two points are worth emphasizing. The first is that the idea of a knowledge society is both problematic and contested. We need to beware of building scenarios and policies for the future development of higher education on the apparently solid ground of a shared understanding of the direction of social change. There can be no such solid ground, because there is no shared understanding. The second is that the university is implicated in all these different meanings of the knowledge society; for example, as the source of the basic science from which highly sophisticated information and communication technologies (and bio- and nano-technologies) are derived; as a 'national' institution (because, despite their internationalist rhetoric, universities are creatures of the nation state) threatened by the decay of the welfare states that have nourished their development and challenged by market-led globalization; and as critical institutions from which alternative, even oppositional, ideologies emerge. So the university itself may have become a problematic and contested institution.

NEW PATTERNS OF KNOWLEDGE PRODUCTION

This conclusion receives further support from an analysis of changes in knowledge production. These have been characterized by Michael Gibbons and others as a shift from so-called 'Mode One' science – basic research driven by scientific curiosity, undertaken in universities (or similar institutions) and 'policed' by self-sustaining scientific communities – to 'Mode Two' knowledge – generated within much more open contexts of application (and implication), socially distributed across a range of actors and environments, and steered by complex evaluation and accountability regimes (Gibbons et al., 1994). Helga Nowotny, Michael Gibbons and the present author have attempted to develop (and defend) this account of knowledge production. In their most recent book a clear distinction has been drawn between what is termed the 'contextualization' of science and crude social-constructionist accounts, one of the main criticisms of the Mode One/Two account. This book also develops the concepts of the *agora*, that wider part-political, part-market, part-cultural domain in which research is reflexively shaped, contested and absorbed (Nowotny et al., 2001).

There is not room in this paper on the impact of globalization on the university to enter more deeply into these debates about how best to conceptualize changes in knowledge production. But the conclusion that can be drawn from the Mode One/Two account, and also 'rival' accounts such as the idea of the Triple Helix (university, industry and state) developed by people such as Henry Etkowitz (1997), is that it is misleading to see these changes as evidence of a kind of linear paradigm shift from an 'old economy' of pure science and disinterested scholarship to a 'new economy' of applied science and activist research. That is not what is happening, for two main reasons. First, the various 'modes' of knowledge production co-exist (and even collaborate). Second, these new patterns of knowledge production cannot crudely be reduced to programmatic and outcome-oriented research. National R&D programmes, we would argue, are not good examples of what we mean by 'contextualized', or socially distributed, research. So, as with the idea of the knowledge society, accounts of changes in scientific production do not provide us with the firm foundations on which we can build secure scenarios about the future development of higher education. Also, as with the knowledge society, the university is complexly embroiled – as the producer of (most) basic science; but also as an increasingly aggressive exploiter of intellectual property and as the mediator (or broker) of research results.

MARKET CHALLENGES TO THE UNIVERSITY

It is against this background of complexity, even of ambiguity, that the theme of this contribution – the impact of globalization on higher education and, in particular, the emergence of new players in the knowledge society – must be explored. Not only is the path the university should follow far from clear but these new players are not as easy to identify as is commonly supposed. The standard view, which needs to be questioned if not challenged outright, is that the current dominance of universities in the knowledge game (which has never been as complete as is sometimes asserted) is now being challenged by rival knowledge organizations. A range of rival organizations is offered: think-tanks, management consultants (now with their 'Centres for Business Knowledge'), the mass media, scenario-planners in major corporations and so on. Of course, the degree of rivalry can easily be exaggerated. As most of these supposed rivals depend crucially on universities for their highly educated graduate workforces, and because the 'research' they generate is often parasitic upon, or deeply enmeshed in, university research, it is not clear that their existence can necessarily be regarded as a challenge to the leading position of the universities; rather it could be regarded as a reinforcement of that position.

However, typically three major rivals are identified by the ever-increasing number of 'observatories' that have been established:

- The first is the development of so-called 'borderless education' institutions (Committee of Vice-Chancellors…, 2000).[1] Some of these are based on global consortia of traditional universities, or mixed consortia of world-class universities (world-class because the 'brand' is all important in this arena) and global corporations, either mass media or IT. Others, of course, are more directly rivals to the traditional universities and may take the form of on-line 'universities' established by such corporations. The fundamental analysis underlying all these efforts is that the problem is not the development of intellectual concepts and content – which can either be bought off-the-peg or provided by academic entrepreneurs/sub-contractors as part of a supply-chain – but the customization, delivery and marketing of these intellectual 'products', the potential of which is now massively enhanced by the power of information and communication technologies. However, this analysis is not overwhelmingly convincing. It is rooted in a one-dimensional technology-deterministic account of the knowledge society; it ignores the complexities of cultural transfer and of 'local' takes on 'global' knowledge (and consequently is restricted in its operation to a narrow range of disciplines: overwhelmingly business and management, IT and computer science, and some fields of science and engineering); and it fails to understand the synergies and complementarities between traditional face-to-face and 'virtual' forms of learning.
- The second group of rival institutions comprises private for-profit 'universities'. The University of Phoenix is the inevitable totemic example, but there are several others. These institutions, because they are in the private sector, are – apparently – unencumbered by the burden of state and public regulation and, therefore, free to operate more entrepreneu-

rially. The qualification 'apparently' is necessary because, since the collapse of Enron and other high-profile corporate scandals, the degree of scrutiny over the private sector is inevitably (and rightly) increasing. Also the experience of privatization, certainly in Europe, has been to increase rather than to reduce the regulatory burden. In addition, private for-profit 'universities' like Phoenix, because they are not universities at all in a traditional sense, are also unencumbered by the burden of intellectual, professional and cultural norms that 'proper' universities, public (not-for-profit) or private, have to carry. This may be a genuine advantage or, better, difference. Such institutions are free to unbundle activities such as research and teaching, course design and course delivery; nor do they need to worry about disciplines as communities of intellect, because they are able to concentrate simply on knowledge 'products'. But many of the constraints that apply to 'borderless education' enterprises also apply to private for-profit universities. In addition the analysis that animates their existence is again rooted in a one-dimensional account of the knowledge society, the geopolitical triumph of the market state (or, perhaps, just the market).

- The third 'threat' to the traditional university is seen as coming from the proliferation of 'corporate universities' (Kenney-Wallace, 2000).[2] Sometimes these take the form of rebadged company training departments, perhaps with some R&D elements thrown in. This kind of development has been encouraged and legitimized by the growth of a powerful 'human resources' discourse. At other times the establishment of corporate universities reflects a more concerted approach to workforce development. A good example is the recent formation in the United Kingdom of the 'National Health Service University'.[3] However, although both are important developments, it is far from clear that either can be accurately represented as a challenge to the traditional university. First, many 'corporate universities' are engaged in lower-level training and/or short-course-based continuing professional development; they often contract with universities for the provision of more sophisticated courses. Second, their activities are largely complementary to those of existing universities. For example, the NHS University is not going to set up in competition with university medical schools, or even schools of nursing.

While all three categories of rival organization – 'borderless education' institutions, private for-profit 'universities' and 'corporate universities' – will be prominent features of the twenty-first-century higher education landscape, they will not necessarily be the most prominent – and certainly not the most interesting – features of that landscape. The reason is that, just as it is wrong to treat the idea of a knowledge society or changes in knowledge production as linear shifts – the replacement of one paradigm by another (superior?) paradigm in the stately march of 'progress' – so it is misleading to see the evolution of the University solely in terms of the 'other', the emergence of rival institutions. It is necessary to develop a much more subtle account, one which places as much emphasis on the process of 'internal' transformation as 'external' challenge (or substitution).

OTHER CHALLENGES: HYBRIDIZATION AND 'ACTIVIST' KNOWLEDGE ORGANIZATIONS

It is necessary to look for new players in the knowledge society not only outside but also deep inside the university itself. In particular two phenomena deserve to be emphasized: one internal to the university, which I will call the hybridization of higher education; and the other external to it, the development of 'alternative' knowledge organizations espousing rival knowledge traditions, which are radical in their political orientation and postmodern in their intellectual orientation (and which may be just as important at the market-based rivals to the public university).

The hybridization of higher education takes two forms. The first is part of the developmental process of modern higher education systems. Institutions take on an increasingly wide and eclectic range of functions, many of which are very distant from the core purposes of the traditional university (although it is necessary to exercise great care not to take the rhetoric of the traditional university, whether derived from John Henry Newman or Robert Hutchins, as necessarily offering a good description of those core purposes). This phenomenon is best described as mission spread or, better, mission stretch because it has not been a process imposed from outside higher education on unwilling institutions but is one that also arises from the interior social and scientific dynamics of higher education. These new functions – technology transfer and knowledge management, social inclusion and lifelong learning – are familiar to everyone. But it is misleading to regard them simply as add-ons. The nature of teaching and learning, of academic courses, of research programmes has also been transformed. There are now open frontiers between the academy and society, the economy and culture. Work-based and community learning, the accreditation of prior experience and similar practices and phenomena are evidence of such cross-frontier flows. So, if we ask who are the new players, the answer is – in part – ourselves: universities themselves are the new players.

The second form taken by the hybridization of higher education is an extension of the first. It is the emergence of new organizational forms within the university that parallel (and rival?) traditional patterns of academic organization such as faculties and departments. Of course, that traditional taxonomy has complex origins: some parts are based on academic affinities and are 'policed' by (fairly) coherent scientific communities; other parts reflect the division of professional labour in wider society (although this division of labour has not been imposed on the university from the outside; law schools and medical schools play a key role not only in the reproduction but also in the definition of professions). It is difficult to claim that research institutes or graduate schools are novel forms (especially, of course, in North America). However, the balance is now changing. More and more organizational units within universities are based on neither principle: academic affinities or the division of professional (or expert) labour. Instead they have more in common with project teams, think-tanks, task-forces – and, of course, market entities designed to exploit the intellectual property that is generated within the university. These old and new organizational forms coexist, sometimes as rivals but at other times as allies. Again, if we ask where are the new organizations in the knowledge society, the answer – in part – is again ourselves: universities are creating many of these new organizations (Clark, 1998).

The second phenomenon is the potential for growing 'activist' knowledge organizations that are in opposition to both traditional universities and to the new 'market' universities. They are opposed to traditional universities because they associate them (us) with social elitism (or the reproduction of social hierarchies according to the division of labour in a capitalist society) and also with restrictive definitions of knowledge that again are elitist, frequently still gendered (despite the impact of feminism) and generally dismissive of alternative and popular knowledge traditions. As a result these 'activist' knowledge organizations challenge notions of evidence, objectivity, balance and debate that have typically been regarded as fundamental to the university (even if these high ideals have not always been met).

However, these organizations are equally opposed to the 'market' universities, which are usually taken to be the principal rivals of the public university. They reject many of the 'givens' that most of us have been bullied into accepting in this (apparent) twilight of social democracy and the welfare state: the materiality of motivation, the efficacy of incentives, the drive to efficiency, the calculus of cost and benefits (on which, of course, the case for developing 'market' universities is based). And, paradoxically, they reject these 'givens' while taking full advantage of the technologies of mass communication that we take to be typical of the market economy.

These 'activist' knowledge organizations take many forms, from local community groups, now with access to global data-bases and communication networks, through fundamentalists of all kinds, perhaps even to global terrorist networks. (However difficult it is to accept the notion that terrorist or extremist organizations are also knowledge organizations, they employ sophisticated technologies and develop their own ideologies.) These organizations also range from fundamentalists, which fundamentally reject the culture of liberality associated with elite universities and the parallel culture of rationality associated with university science and scholarship, to organizations such as Greenpeace, which believe with some justice that their rational use of scientific evidence is equal or superior to that of the World Bank or the International Monetary Fund (IMF). The controversy over genetically modified food is a good example of how expertise is no longer the preserve of recognized 'experts' but is now much more widely distributed. It is also a good example of the creative role that such controversies play in the generation of new knowledge. At their best these 'activist' knowledge organizations, in their enthusiasm for a more democratic distribution of knowledge resources and their opposition to the more baleful aspects of globalization, may be assuming some of the ethical responsibilities that universities willingly accepted a generation ago but from which they have more recently distanced themselves.

CONCLUSION

Familiar accounts of the emergence of new players in the knowledge society (and, therefore, potential rivals to the university), which emphasize the challenge from 'market' organizations such as private for-profit and corporate universities, are unsatisfactory and inadequate. These accounts are based on a naïve and one-dimensional interpretation of the knowledge society, which in fact is a problematical category with multiple, and contested, interpretations. Furthermore these accounts attach too little weight to the fundamental – but, again, complex and ambiguous – changes that are taking place in knowledge production. As a result too much emphasis has been placed on immediate and obvious rivals to the university, and too little on the transformation of modern higher education systems – mission stretch and hybridization – and on the challenges presented by non-market rivals which embrace a multitude of alternative 'activist' knowledge institutions. It is only when all three sets of new players – 'market' rivals to public universities, non-market challengers and new organizational forms within the university itself – are considered that a comprehensive picture of the stake-holders in the knowledge society can emerge.

NOTES

1. Up-to-date information on borderless and distance education can be found on http://www.obhe.ac.uk/
2. Further information on corporate universities is available on http://www.corpu.com/
3. Up-to-date information on the National Health Service University is available on http://www.doh.gov.uk/nhsuniversity/

BIBLIOGRAPHY

Beck, U. 1992. *Risk Society: Towards a New Modernity*. London, Sage.

Bobbitt, P. 2002. *The Shield of Achilles: War, Peace and the Course of History*. London, Allen Lane.

Castells, M. 1996, 1997, 1998. *The Information Age: Economy, Society and Culture* (Vol. 1: *The Rise of Network Society*; Vol. 2: *The Power of Identity*; Vol. 3: *End of Millennium*). Oxford, Blackwell.

Clark, B. 1998. *Creating Entrepreneurial Universities: Organizational Pathways of Transformation*. Oxford, Pergamon. (published on behalf of the International Association of Universities.)

Committee of Vice-Chancellors and Principals and Higher Education Funding Council for England. 2000. *The Business of Borderless Education: UK Perspectives – Summary Report*. London, CVCP.

Etzkowitz, H. and Leydesdorff, L. (eds). 1997. *Universities and the Global Knowledge Economy: A Triple Helix of University–Industry–Government Relations*. London, Pinter.

Fukuyama, F. 1992. *The End of History and the Last Man*. London, Penguin.

Gibbons, M., Limoges, C., Nowotny, H., Schwartzman, S., Scott, P. and Trow, M. 1994. *The New Production of Knowledge: The Dynamics of Science and Research in Contemporary Societies*. London, Sage.

Kennedy, P. 1988. *The Rise and Fall of Great Powers*. New York, Random House.

——.1993. *Preparing for the Twenty-first Century*. New York, Random House.

Kenney-Wallace, G. 2000. Plato.com: The Role and Impact of Corporate Universities in the Third Millennium. In P. Scott, *Higher Education-Reformed*. London, Falmer.

Lyotard, J.-F. 1984. *The Postmodern Condition: A Report on Knowledge*. Manchester, Manchester University Press. (Originally published by Les Éditions de Minuit in 1979.)

Nowotny, H., Gibbons, M. and Scott, P. 2001. *Re-Thinking Science: Knowledge and the Public in an Age of Uncertainty*. Cambridge, Polity.

Conclusion
Universities and Globalization: In Search of a New Balance

François Tavenas

SOME COMMENTS ON GLOBALIZATION

The authors of this book have stressed the difficulties associated today with the term 'globalization', which covers a vast number of interpretations and generates emotional and often not very rational reactions, to the point where the term is becoming a problem in itself. It is important that universities develop a better definition of this concept and share it with their students and society as a whole. As John Daniel (Chapter 1) and Chris Brooks (Chapter 2) aptly point out, globalization is neither the supreme evil, the cause of all problems, which must be destroyed at all costs, nor is it the unique and ideal path towards prosperity, a path which should be followed blindly. In its current form, globalization has many positive aspects that must be promoted, such as the direct access to unfiltered and uncensored information thanks to the Internet. However, it also has very negative aspects that must be changed. For example, its analytical framework is focused too narrowly on financial considerations and not enough on cultural and social considerations, leading to growing disparities between countries and even between citizens of the same country. Globalization is a phenomenon that presents humanity with problems as well as opportunities, a phenomenon that must be studied, understood and managed so that it will lead to a global interdependence and generate progress that is equitable for all nations and all citizens of the world.

As John Daniel rightly reminds us, referring to the state of the world economy in the early twentieth century, globalization is not as new a phenomenon for our societies and the world economy as we would like to think. It is certainly not new for universities. Indeed, globalization has always been an integral part of university life, ever since the University of Bologna was created and its members were granted safe-conducts by Emperor Friedrich Barbarossa to move freely within medieval Europe. John Daniel reminds us further of the examples of Erasmus, a professor active in all the great universities of Europe in his time, and of those unruly English students who created Oxford University after being expelled from the Sorbonne. We need only recall the international mobility of researchers that has always existed, the role of international learned societies in all disciplines of knowledge, and the role of international academic journals and large international conferences as preferred means to disseminate research results; all of this is proof that the practice of globalization is well established in academic communities.

However, what is new is the extent of the current phenomenon of globalization, that is, the growing interdependence of all societies and all segments of each society; the accelerating pace of the movement of ideas, goods and people; the emergence of the phenomenon of local decisions having a global impact; the increasing complexity and uncertainty of the world and its mechanisms; and of course, the impact of the Internet whose effects we are barely beginning to grasp. We need to better understand the consequences of this evolution so that we can adapt to it, but also and especially, so that we can master it and guide it in a direction that is conducive to progress for all of humanity.

The fact that the world is evolving towards globalization poses two types of problems for higher education: problems related to our teaching and research mission – how to adapt our teaching programmes and which new research fields to open – and problems linked with our organization and our institutional policies and strategies.

ISSUES RELATED TO TRAINING AND RESEARCH PROGRAMMES

Of all the issues facing us brought up by the various authors, I would like to consider three in particular.

- First, educational institutions have the dual mission to develop and transmit knowledge and universal values and, at the same time, to contribute to the cultural, economic and social development of the local societies that they serve and that support them. Thus, for each university, the challenge is to find the right balance between these two sometimes contradictory missions. This challenge is all the greater since it must be taken up in a context where knowledge is recognized as a factor critical to economic development, and thus regarded by governments and all social players as a means to ensure a competitive advantage to any nation in a globalized world. Universities are thus subject to contradictory pressures: on the one hand, their internal tradition of 'scientific communism' encourages them to promote the free movement of ideas and people internationally; on the other hand, governments and society, which provide the bulk of their financial resources, expect a return on this investment in the form of contributions to local economic development. In the coming years, finding the right balance between our universal and local missions will be an increasingly challenging task.

- Second, the world of higher education is still living under the 'tyranny' of scientific disciplines and sub-disciplines. To use the terminology proposed by Michael Gibbons (Chapter 6), 'Mode One' governs our internal structures of faculties and departments, our external structures of knowledge diffusion (learned societies, academic journals), our practices of merit recognition (criteria for hiring and promotion, remuneration of professors, academic awards and distinctions), and our teaching and research programmes. Nevertheless, the problems facing humanity are increasingly complex and transdisciplinary. As Gibbons and several other contributors point out, there is an urgent need to adapt to 'Mode Two' knowledge production by introducing an increasing transdisciplinary dimension into our practices. These should include:
  - new programmes and new structures that are flexible, transdisciplinary and centred on problem-solving (the flexible matrix structure suggested by Hans van Ginkel in Chapter 4 offers one such approach);
  - new systems for recognizing merit, for both professors and institutions, which would put less emphasis on disciplinary merits and give more importance to multi- and interdisciplinary contributions; and
  - new programmes, or new activities within existing programmes, to give our students greater access to transdisciplinary dimensions and, hence, a training that is more in keeping with the demands of the complex world in which they live.

- Third, the mission of higher education is to train tomorrow's social actors and leaders. These people will have to work in an increasingly complex world and deal with more and more complicated problems. Our programmes must be adapted so as to better prepare them to take up this challenge by developing new capacities:
  - learning to learn;
  - understanding global and transdisciplinary issues;
  - interacting with different social groups: specialists in all fields, citizens often not equipped to understand complex issues, legislators, etc.
  - understanding and capacity to act in varied cultural environments; it is by developing students' international mobility, and especially North–South mobility, that this capacity will be most effectively developed; and
  - more generally, simultaneous acquisition of universal values and functional and professional knowledge of high quality.

ISSUES RELATING TO OUR INSTITUTIONS, THEIR STRUCTURES AND POLICIES

Not only does globalization have a major impact on all universities, but this impact is felt in many ways in terms of structures, procedures and institutional policies. Six key points emerge:

- First, the Internet is radically transforming access to information. The traditional roles of a university professor as a source of knowledge and of the campus as the unique place for the transmission of this knowledge, are being strongly challenged. While we can certainly attempt to resist this evolution, it would be at our peril. I think that we must, on the contrary, embrace the Internet and adapt to it in several ways:
  - Refocusing the role of university professors as mentor, adviser and guide to students in the search, analysis, criticism and integration of the information available on the Web and elsewhere: this role is vital and must be developed given, as we all know, the amount of nonsense which co-exists with quality information on the Web.
  - Following the example of MIT, using the Internet to disseminate quality academic material freely and to the broadest public possible; we must be aware that this approach, which is entirely consistent with our tradition of the free movement of ideas, will also open up our pedagogical material to an informal but global system of peer

assessment, with all the consequences that this may carry for the
reputation of individual professors as well as institutions.
- Using the Internet as a means to increase considerably cooperation
  between universities and to facilitate new research partnerships; the
  benefits for universities in countries of the South could be quite
  substantial.

• Second, globalization and accelerating knowledge production require
  that universities rapidly increase their delivery of continuing education
  programmes. However, with a few notable exceptions, universities have
  generally paid only lip-service to this area.

Continuing education must be integrated into the university's central
missions rather than being confined, as is too often the case, to parallel
if not external structures. The Internet provides us with an extraor-
dinary tool to deliver, everywhere and 'just-in-time', updated knowledge
to our graduates to help them deal with career shifts and new professional challenges; we should exploit this new tool to assume our
responsibilities fully.

Continuing education is a highly competitive business area in which most
of the new higher education players are found, including for-profit organizations. Therefore, universities must clearly define their fields of action
in order to be successful in this competitive environment. They should
probably concentrate on their fundamental mission of developing
knowledge and people by providing continuing education to their graduates
rather than by being guided by commercial or financial criteria only.

• Third, the main concern of the international academic community
  should be to fight against the widening of the knowledge gap between
  developed and emerging nations, so as to prevent the creation of what
  Teboho Moja (Chapter 11) calls 'global apartheid'. Many contributors
  have emphasized the potential benefits, but also the great dangers,
  associated with the growth of interventions by foreign suppliers of
  higher education services in developing countries. The issues raised by
  our colleagues Moja and Mohamedbhai (Chapter 10) should be carefully
  examined, especially the danger that these foreign suppliers will prevent
  local institutions from developing by creating unfair competition in the
  recruitment of students, professors and administrators.

New forms of university cooperation must be established. In particular, Michael Gibbons' proposal to develop 'twinning' between universities of the North and the South deserves careful consideration in as much as we all seem to agree that this would offer potential for concrete and much more effective development than the cooperation models implemented thus far by the large international organizations. UNESCO and our international associations could play a constructive role in developing this approach.

- Fourth, the issue of funding higher education is extremely complex and unfortunately does not have a simple solution. I would not dare draw a conclusion from everything that was said during our discussions, but I think that there is enough subject matter on this issue for another conference and that it should be organized soon.

I would simply like to emphasize that the real issue is the quality of education and the capacity of each society to mobilize the financial resources needed to ensure this quality. A secondary issue is to determine how to share these financial resources among the various social players: students, governments (and through them the general public) and businesses. Unfortunately, this latter issue has tended to monopolize most political debates, with misinformation often contributing to its superficiality. We must refocus our discussions on the vital issue of the means necessary to deliver quality higher education and on the best ways to ensure wide as well as equitable accessibility to all those who have the ability and the desire to acquire a university education and then to contribute effectively to societal development. We must also try to be objective and rigorous in this debate so as to avoid the pitfalls of demagogy.

- Fifth, competitive approaches to relations between universities are probably more harmful than beneficial, if they are assessed in the light of our traditional values of the free movement of ideas and people. We have seen how competition for students, professors and managers contributes to the brain drain and the widening gap between countries of the North and the South, thus worsening a situation which we should instead be attempting to improve. Jan Currie (Chapter 12) illustrates to what extent competitive and commercial approaches can produce questionable results, sometimes creating very serious difficulties for the universities which adopt them. Of course, there are outstanding successes such as that of the University of Phoenix (Chapter 13) in a well-defined field of action, but at the same time there are many failures that are just as noteworthy.

If we truly want to protect the traditional values of higher education, namely the free movement of ideas and people and the contribution to the production of universal knowledge for the benefit of all humanity, we must chart the course of our actions on the basis of these values, that is, on cooperative rather than competitive approaches.

* Sixth, and last, this leads us to the central issue of higher education and the GATS agreements. We have established a very clear consensus that higher education is not merchandise whose international trade should be regulated according to the same mechanisms as the trade in wood, petroleum or planes. This does not mean that higher education should be excluded from all global trade regulation systems, but rather that it should be governed by its own very specific set of rules.

Riccardo Petrella (Chapter 8) passionately appeals to us to challenge the fundamental aspects of globalization as we are experiencing it today; this is a matter for serious thought in the medium and long term. However, we must deal with an immediate situation in which, as is clearly pointed out by Jane Knight (Chapter 5), the GATS negotiations are developed between governments without universities having made their positions on the issue known. Academic communities urgently need to take charge of this matter and make their positions known to their government representatives in order to avoid inadvertent but irreparable mistakes.

To formulate these positions, we must seriously examine all aspects of the issue. This has begun in various places, but we must intensify our efforts by referring to the joint declaration adopted in September 2001 by the Association of Universities and Colleges of Canada, the American Council on Education, the European University Association and the Council for Higher Education Accreditation (see Appendix).

As Pascal noted, 'la nature a horreur du vide'. This is also true of the international community. It is not enough for us to say that 'we do not want the GATS'. We must say how we want to organize the international space of higher education. No doubt, our collective authorities – IAU, AUC, AUF – have a role to play in this. UNESCO can also play a role by helping us set up an international space based on the principles of the free movement of ideas and people, of contribution to the production of universal knowledge, of participation in the process of acculturation of people, and of the cultural, economic and social development of societies that are served by the universities.

As a former Quebec minister and former president of the Board of Directors of Université Laval recently said: 'I would be happy to live in the global village, but where is the City Hall?' (translation). We need to have a municipal council, or rather an international academic assembly, a 'gatekeeper', to use the expression of Hans van Ginkel, to deal with the central issues of the quality of higher education, recognition of diplomas, protection of the cultural and social relevance of national systems of higher education, and promotion of international university cooperation.

CONCLUSION

I believe that these are the main conclusions and courses of action that have emerged from the authors' contributions. To conclude, I would like to leave you with two thoughts that sum up both our action and our challenge. The first, which should always guide our actions as academics, comes from Einstein:

Concern for man himself must always constitute the chief objective of all technological effort.

The second, which we owe to Deming, should always be kept in mind in these times of permanent and rapid change:

Change is mandatory, survival is optional; choose wisely.

NOTE

This paper is a written version of the conclusions I gave at the conference on *Globalization: What Issues are at Stake for Universities?* 18–21 September 2002 at Université Laval, Quebec, Canada.

Postscript
Higher Education:
Social Relevance and Collective Action

On the basis of the analyses we have just read, it is not possible to say whether the ongoing globalization process will be self-limiting or, on the contrary, will continue to expand, thereby creating more upheaval in higher education. We believe that the preceding panoramic view of the challenges faced by universities has shown that the answer to this question largely depends on the action of the people and institutions involved. Despite their diverse approaches and perspectives, the authors agree on numerous themes and at least on the fact that the *role* of universities, even though it has changed during the past few decades, is still to produce and transmit knowledge. What seems to have emerged from these texts and this 'snap shot' is that universities are at a turning point in their history in terms of their *place* within society. From a place of being a universal conscience – which they have not taken on for decades and which they could claim on the grounds of their religious origins – universities can, in our view, move on to the place of social actor. Today, international society needs this actor in order to deal with the enormous challenges raised by the increasingly worrying situation of the academic world in the countries of the South and by the fact that knowledge has become an object in the countries of the North. Indeed, the debate cannot be reduced to deciding between a world of higher education governed by international trade criteria and a 'protected' or 'exempted' world. The question is whether universities in the North and the South are willing to, first, embrace a global university logic, which implies viewing the world in its entirety, and, second, take on, as institutions and not only as a community of academics, their rightful place within 'international civil society' so that they may, third, take charge of the regulation of the international space of higher education for which they are responsible and which is opening up to them due to the effects of globalization.

EMBRACING A GLOBAL UNIVERSITY LOGIC

For at least a century, the university has been defined as a national institution, funded partly or wholly by a political entity (a state, a region, a province, a *Land*). The university works on knowledge that is essentially universal and, through its permanent relationship with numerous foreign partners, considers itself to be international. The reality is quite different. This international world is basically bilateral and largely dominated by relations between developed countries among which students and professors communicate and ultimately conduct exchanges under mobility programmes. The other countries, known as Southern countries, are not part of the world of academic exchanges.[1] They are limited to being recipients of assistance programmes and/or individual initiatives of students, programmes, departments or else – although more rarely – faculties. While these programmes and initiatives rival each other in imagination, generosity and know-how, there is unfortunately no coordination between them.

However, globalization clearly shows that there are indeed two worlds, no longer only a world of poor countries and a world of rich countries – distinguished only by wealth or lack of it – but a world also split in two by exclusion.[2] It is useful to examine this quite recent concept briefly, since our construct conjures up more easily the image of the poor who simply do not possess any private property. Exclusion is a broader concept because it implies the notion of exclusion from society and, in particular, from public goods (health, security, freedom, education, dignity, water and electricity) which, in our hemisphere, are accessible even to the poor. In the globalized world of universities, exclusion may mean that it is impossible for students in poor countries to have access to higher education of any sort – let alone education of really high quality – or even to information. Similarly, it may be impossible for professors to renew themselves, to educate themselves, or to participate in colloquiums and conferences abroad. While we have sometimes opened our hearts and shown our compassion, today it is important to open our eyes so that we can go beyond merely helping this other academic world to take action and instead to integrate it.

A complete examination of relations between universities in the North and the South is in order. The onus is on us as an international academic community – which knows so well how to revile private enterprise for acting out of self-interest – to examine the crucial issues that are emerging. In particular, will universities in the North continue to rob the Southern countries of their most qualified work force through their entirely self-interested policy of recruiting foreign students (See Introduction)? Moreover, are we going to entrust the regulation of higher education in more than 150 countries to the only international trade regulating authority, the World Trade Organization (WTO)? Viewing the academic world as global means respecting the national system to which we belong while constructing a space that fosters exchanges with countries in the South.

TAKING UP OUR PLACE WITHIN 'INTERNATIONAL CIVIL SOCIETY'

The second point that we would like to raise here relates to the *place* of universities in a modern society. The word place is emphasized here to distinguish it from the *role* of the university, which was mentioned earlier. The place of the university has changed over the ages. It is not our intention to trace the genealogy of the university's place within society but rather to focus on the present situation. In referring to the university or universities and their place, an introductory remark is in order. The university is one of the oldest institutions. We talk and debate about it, judge and criticize it, give roles and assign a place to it without it saying anything at all! What we mean is that the university as an institution barely expresses itself. It is still mainly a community of professors who are loath to identify themselves with an institution that essentially dissolves individualities in the general interest. In this respect, the internationalization of universities is a good example. In the majority of cases, it is the projects of professors and students that have brought about partnerships among universities. The university as an institution rarely expresses its will, especially when this involves choices with an ethical connotation such as that of participating in international cooperation programmes. Instead there is a mosaic of ad hoc and limited expressions of the university's policy, as if all of these stands could reflect the institution's will. This situation is due to the very nature of the status of university professors, who consider their Rector or President to be an administrator and never a representative of the academic community's fundamental thinking. Hence the current place of the university in national civil society is vague, uncertain and often changing. Furthermore its behaviour is often muted and unassertive regarding the important issues facing countries. In contrast, the place of academics in society is quite clear. Despite a less satisfactory financial situation than that of their colleagues in the private sector, they are high on the social scale, admired, recognized and even sometimes envied![3] Audacity is not part of the institution's vocabulary; it may be, at best, the prerogative of certain individuals who risk their career in it. The place of universities at the national level could be caricatured by the image of a touring theatre actor who is always running after the troupe in which he was supposed to play. Universities most often follow, and react to all new phenomena with some reservation and a distance that allows them to take a step back to gain the needed perspective. The problem is that history is accelerating and universities cannot by themselves slow down time.

The real challenge is to determine the place of universities within 'international civil society'. Before addressing this question, it is useful to identify what is included in the expression 'international civil society'. Given the polysemic nature of the concept, the meaning put forward by Béatrice Pouligny will be used here.[4] According to Pouligny, international civil society means the emergence of new actors who claim to be experts in a certain cause or theme and whose representativeness is not derived from the number of their constituents but from the legitimacy of the cause that they defend. In a more realistic and even cynical manner, we think that the governments of industrialized countries, which are experiencing a loss of interest in public matters and growing problems of representativeness within their national territory, have found in these emergent new actor-experts the means to establish a dialogue with intermediary bodies that represent the general interest and not the sum of all corporatist interests that national representation henceforth constitutes. Similarly, at the international level, states often found themselves in headlong confrontations with national interests. The emergence of these global actors, who are cosmopolitan experts originating from the same elitist networks, have given governments as well as international institutions the feeling of having new actors working close to the ground and bringing a vision other than that of policies to the debate. This is how, from the mid-twentieth century onwards, in relative transparency, the company, as a new creator of employment, became a world social actor. Despite its for-profit vocation, it successfully took its social place *vis-à-vis* the millions of employees throughout the world for whom it had provided jobs. The other actors of international civil society have naturally found their places on the same basis, that is, representing issues that concern the entire planet, the environment, health and human rights.

We believe that universities have their place on the international scene as new world social actors. The forming of a society for which knowledge is the raw material strengthens the idea that the twenty-first century will be the century of work and not the century of employment. It is individuals who will create their own employment by supplying work that will involve more and more imagination, creation and freedom, as opposed to jobs that used to impose the fulfilment of a repetitive task and the enslavement of human beings. While the company has been the key social actor of the twentieth century by *providing millions of jobs to people*, universities can be the world social actor of the twenty-first century by *permiting millions of students to find a job* inasmuch as these universities are willing – through appropriate teaching programmes – to give their students the means to take their place in this new world of work. Universities possess the knowledge, the discourse and the quality of researchers/professors required, and their legitimacy is based on knowledge, the raw material of the new society. They also possess a competency in the transmission of knowledge that can turn them into informed mediators between governments and citizens.

HOW SHOULD THE GLOBAL SPACE OF HIGHER EDUCATION BE REGULATED?

Before attempting to show that the structuring of a new global space of higher education will henceforth both be in the interest of universities and enhance their social responsibility, we should first report on the situation to date. The current attitude of the majority of universities on the international scene can be summed up in a single word – individualism. By this we mean that there is a glaring absence of university representation as institutions on the international scene. Each university lives for itself and by itself in a context of common indifference. Though this may seem strange for institutions that rely on 'epistemic communities', it relates to something referred to earlier, that is, the little weight that the institution carries as compared to the influence of the community of professors. Thus, of the approximately 16,000 universities and colleges surveyed in the world (IAU/UNESCO, 2002), no more than 1,600 (adjusted for dual memberships) belong to an international association such as the International Association of Universities (IAU), the International Association of University Presidents (IAUP, which is more of a club for university presidents in the North) or the Association of Commonwealth Universities (ACU). This apparent lack of interest simply reflects the fact that universities only belong to a national association or conference of rectors/presidents when there is something in it for them, that is, as a means to deal with their natural interlocutor, the state. This reasoning also applies to regional organizations, particularly the European Union, which has established a higher education policy endowed with the necessary funds; hence the attractiveness of the European Association of Universities. These organizations have a clear role: 'to defend the interests' of their members. In contrast, the international associations mentioned above – whose work, it should be mentioned, is exemplary – are in a delicate situation, for they must avoid encroaching on both national and regional affairs. Thus, membership in these associations is Utopian for the most pragmatic, while for others it is an act of pure faith. An initial, recent consequence of this quasi-inexistent representation of the academic world at the global level is that higher education has been placed on the agenda of the General Agreement on Trade in Services (Knight, Chapter 5), which means that the 144 member countries of the WTO have been given responsibility for negotiating the future of higher education as a service in the same way as electronic data processing or transportation.

For this reason, we maintain that problems in higher education no longer concern only national or even regional education policy issues but now have global significance. The new global space of higher education must be structured by the universities themselves, which operate it throughout the world. It is not our intention here either to praise existing organizations or to put them on trial but rather to observe that, for reasons to which we will return below, universities are generally absent from the international education scene. There is no doubt that this absence can be partly, but not entirely, explained by the influence of governments on national education systems. Membership in an association, group or movement involves leaving matters in the hands of a person, council or committee, for the explicit purpose of being represented. This membership is generally based on a tacit agreement according to whose terms the member seeks greater expertise than its own in the group, to which, in exchange, it entrusts the task of representing it.

It was mentioned earlier that the academic community is uneasy about giving a mandate to its institution. Therefore, are universities as institutions reluctant to entrust some group with the task of representing them on questions related to their existence and place in the world? Who could possibly claim to be more expert than the university? This question is at the intersection within the university of two currents that have studiously avoided one another: on the one hand, the propensity to lean on the notion of the institution of the university as a constitutive community that is different from any other and, on the other, a real reluctance, even a refusal, to undertake any form of collective action that could result in its dissolution. In our opinion, this is the source of the universities' indecision.

As long as national preoccupations prevailed, the absence of universities and their resistance from any form of collective action did not have direct consequences. However, in 2003, globalization is deterritorializing the issues challenging universities, making it necessary for them to have interlocutors other than nation states. It is therefore becoming essential for universities, as institutions, to realize that it is their responsibility to take part in the global debate on higher education. This no longer means defending the interests of the universities of a particular country or region. Rather, all universities must find and implement the best means to allow the universities of the South to meet the higher education needs of their countries, instead of allowing past errors to be repeated through culpable neglect.

In conclusion, we believe that the global space of higher education deserves the attention of all universities in the world, particularly the most prestigious ones, which – often wrongly – think of themselves as larger than life and therefore feel impelled to go it alone. The recent initiative taken by MIT to make all its course contents accessible and free should be welcomed and encouraged. However, it is easy to imagine that such initiatives, which concern not only each institution but the entire planet, could carry even more weight and have greater effect if they were the result of a position taken by the community of university institutions rather than by one of the most prestigious universities in the world. This is not to suggest that its practices should be upset or commitments renounced but simply that as social, global actors, we also need to be concerned with structuring a corresponding global space.

Either universities are what we, the academic community, think they are, that is, institutions working for the entire world community, and through our presence we are able to mobilize ourselves to regulate this space; or we continue to be absent and indifferent and remain nothing more than merchants of illusions who have masked our cult of institutional individualism in the virtuous cloaks of an ancient community which some would have liked to represent.

Gilles Breton
Michel Lambert
January 23, 2003

NOTES

1. For a comprehensive study of the Southern countries, see *Higher Education in Developing Countries: Peril and Promise,* The Task Force on Higher Education and Society (eds) Washington D.C., The World Bank, (2000).
2. For the origin of this concept, see Jules Klanfer (1965) *L'Exclusion sociale,* Paris, bureau de recherches sociales; Pierre Massé (1969) *Les dividendes du progrès,* Paris, Le Seuil; René Lenoir (1974) *Les Exclus,* Paris, Le Seuil; or Serge Paugam (1996) (ed.), *L'Exclusion: l'état des savoirs,* Paris, La Découverte.
3. On the place of academics/intellectuals in society, see the humoristic and critical view of David Brooks (2000) *Bobos in Paradise,* New York, Simon & Schuster.
4. For an analysis of the concept, see Béatrice Pouligny (2001) L'émergence d'une 'société civile internationale'? Processus, Acteurs, Enjeux, working paper. http://www.ceri-sciencespo.com/cerifr/cherlist/pouligny.htm

BIBLIOGRAPHY

IAU/UNESCO. 2002. *World List of Universities and Other Institutions of Higher Education.* New York, Palgrave.

Appendix
Joint Declaration on Higher Education and the General Agreement on Trade in Services

LIST OF SIGNATORIES

Association of Universities and Colleges of Canada (AUCC), representing Canada's 92 public and private not-for-profit universities and degree-level colleges;

American Council on Education (ACE), representing 1,800 accredited degree granting colleges and universities in the United States;

European University Association (EUA), representing 30 national Rectors' Conferences and 537 individual universities across the European continent;

Council for Higher Education Accreditation (CHEA), representing 3,000 accredited, degree-granting colleges and universities and 60 recognized institutional and programmatic accreditors in the United States.

INTRODUCTION

The General Agreement on Trade in Services (GATS) is a multilateral, legally enforceable agreement covering international trade in services. Education services, including higher education, are one of the 12 broad sectors included in the agreement. We, the above associations, put forward the following declaration with respect to the GATS and trade in education services:

PRINCIPLES

Whereas:

Higher education exists to serve the public interest and is not a 'commodity', a fact which WTO Member States have recognized through UNESCO and other international or multilateral bodies, conventions, and declarations. The mission of higher education is to contribute to the sustainable development and improvement of society as a whole by: educating highly qualified graduates able to meet the needs of all sectors of human activity; advancing, creating and disseminating knowledge through research; interpreting, preserving, and promoting cultures in the context of cultural pluralism and diversity; providing opportunities for higher learning throughout life; contributing to the development and improvement of education at all levels; and protecting and enhancing civil society by training young people in the values which form the basis of democratic citizenship and by providing critical and detached perspectives in the discussion of strategic choices facing societies[1].

Given this public mandate, authority to regulate higher education must remain in the hands of competent bodies[2] as designated by any given country. Nothing in international trade agreements should restrict or limit this authority in any way.

Education exports must complement, not undermine, the efforts of developing countries to develop and enhance their own domestic higher education systems. While international cooperation and trade in educational services can present opportunities for developing countries to strengthen their human resources, trade rules must not have the effect of imposing models or approaches to higher education on nations or of weakening their own national systems.

The internationalization of higher education is integral to the quality and relevance of the academic endeavour and research mission in the twenty-first century. For most institutions, international trade in higher education is an important component in attaining higher education's mission. For these institutions, education exports such as international student recruitment or the delivery of higher education programs across borders through distance education are part of a broader set of international activities which include faculty and student exchanges, research cooperation and capacity-building initiatives in developing countries.

Quality is a key objective for both domestic provision of higher education and international education exports, irrespective of the mode of delivery. Appropriate quality assurance mechanisms administered by higher education institutions under the competent bodies must exist to ensure that quality is not compromised. These mechanisms need to be transparent and widely understood.

International higher education cooperation must operate under a rules-based regime. WTO Member States have already established mechanisms to achieve this objective, in forums such as UNESCO, including international conventions on the recognition of academic credentials and a network of national information centres on foreign credentials. These mechanisms need to be further developed and their implementation better supported by our respective governments to protect learners.

Higher education differs significantly from most other service sectors, in that because of its public mandate there is typically a high degree of government involvement in higher education provision co-existing with private funding and commercial activities. This public/private mix permeates not only the sector but, indeed, the individual institutions within it.

Public and private higher education systems are intertwined and interdependent. Therefore it is impossible to effectively separate out certain sub-sectors e.g., adult education, or certain types of institutions e.g., 'private providers', for the purposes of the GATS without impacting other parts of the system.

Caution must be exercised before putting the quality, integrity, accessibility and equity of our higher education institutions and systems at risk without obvious benefit.

Transparency and open consultation with affected stakeholders is imperative in the development of effective public policy.

RATIONALE

Given that:

Very little is known about the consequences of including trade in education services in the GATS such as on the quality, access, and equity of higher education, on domestic authority to regulate higher education systems, and on public subsidies for higher education. The potential risks of including higher education in the GATS, as indicated above, could be very significant.

While there are currently some barriers to trade in education services, there does not appear to be a major problem overall. Institutions continue to be able to actively develop exchange agreements, distance education programmes, research collaborations, offshore partnerships etc. to meet their internationalization objectives and contribute to international development. Moreover, many of these barriers appear to be related to the lack of recognition of academic qualifications or concerns over the quality of educational providers; it is therefore unlikely that they will lend themselves to trade policy remedies through the GATS process. Conversely, there are existing mechanisms, such as the Convention on the Recognition of Qualifications Concerning Higher Education in the European Region (Lisbon Convention), open to all states, which are dealing with these issues. There are also national information centers to foster recognition of credentials and vigorous discussions on ways to improve bilateral or multilateral recognition of each other's domestic quality assurance mechanisms.

It is extremely difficult to clearly define which education services are supplied strictly on a commercial basis due to the public-private mix in all systems and within many institutions of higher education.

GATS Article I:3 is recognized as being ambiguous and open to interpretation.[3] While we applaud senior officials in our respective governments for insisting that public service systems are exempted from the agreement based on Article I:3, we do not understand how this conclusion has been reached given the absence of clear, broadly accepted definitions and, more importantly, the fact that the component parts of the system are so inextricably linked. In addition, history shows that exemptions to international agreements such as the GATS tend to be interpreted narrowly by trade dispute tribunals. For these reasons, it seems unrealistic to assume that public education at the tertiary level is exempted from the GATS based on Article I:3.

Many of our respective countries have not undertaken an effective consultation process between trade officials and the organizations representing public and private higher education institutions.[4]

DECLARATION

Operating under these principles, and given these circumstances, the Association of Universities and Colleges of Canada, the American Council on Education, the European University Association, and the Council for Higher Education Accreditation jointly declare that:

Our member institutions are committed to reducing obstacles to international trade in higher education using conventions and agreements outside of a trade policy regime. This commitment includes, but is not limited to improving communications, expanding information exchanges, and developing agreements concerning higher education institutions, programs, degrees or qualifications and quality review practices.

Our respective countries should not make commitments in Higher Education Services or in the related categories of Adult Education and Other Education Services in the context of the GATS. Where such commitments have already been made in 1995, no further ones should be forthcoming.

AUCC, ACE, EUA, and CHEA convey this joint declaration to the Government of Canada, the office of the United States Trade Representative, the European Commission, individual European states that are members of the nascent European Higher Education Area, and all interested Member States of the WTO for their attention.

Date: 28 September, 2001

Robert J. Giroux	David Ward
President, AUCC	President, ACE
Eric Froment	Judith Eaton
President, EUA	President, CHEA

NOTE

1. Taken from UNESCO's 1998 *World Declaration on Higher Education for the Twenty-First Century: Vision and Action*
2. The term 'competent bodies' is used in order to take into account the fact in any given nation, authority for higher education rests with different levels of government, institutions and organizations.
3. Article I:3 is the agreement's exemption of services supplied in the exercise of government authority, where these services are defined as being supplied neither on a commercial basis nor in competition with one or more service suppliers.
4. It should be noted, howewer; that in the case of Canada, there is ongoing dialogue between the federal government and the education sector with respect to the GATS.